Eating in St. Helena
A Generation's Family Favorites
a recipe memoir

CONTENTS

Phoebe Ellsworth

P.O. Box 854
St. Helena CA 94574
ellsworthphoebe@me.com

©2009

Eating in St. Helena

A Generation's Family Favorites

Early morning walks

When chatting about a party or event many ask who was there or who wore what. Usually, my first question is what did you have to eat? I'm a native Californian and grew up in a family that was always entertaining. Our food was "California style," relatively simple and easy to prepare. Summer with all its bounty of vegetables and fruits brought fresh joys in eating.

The idea for this recipe memoir was seeded on early morning walks with **The Walking Women.** For the last 21 years, Monday through Friday at seven am, a group of St. Helena friends gather for a three-mile walk.

Except for Friday, the route is always the same, down Spring Street to Main, across Main to Adams, up Adams to Hudson over to Madrona and then up Madrona to Judie Rogers' house for coffee. Summer Fridays we start at The Farmers' Market and return there for coffee. The rest of the year we start at The Coffee Shop, varying our route each week to explore the streets and paths of St. Helena.

Sylvia Pestoni and Sandy Herrick started the "walking program" and Bev Popko, who along with Sylvia taught at Heritage School in Calistoga, soon joined them. Sylvia and Bev took walking seriously in those days; they also walked during the school lunch hour. Over the years new people have joined the walkers and others leave. Most are long time residents. I was too busy burning the candle at both ends to join The Walkers until 2003.

Naturally, what we eat and cooking are part of every day's chatting - good buys, places to shop, etc. Recipes are shared and memories of favorites come to mind.

The subject of assembling a recipe collection arose – **The Walking Women's Favorite Recipes**. Then one or another would recall a dish made by others. Remember Alice Jones's killer Texas chocolate sheet cake, or Marj's sausage roll, or was it Linda or Sylvia who first made the apple cake. We decided to include more than our small group and the list kept growing.

Eventually, letters went to more than 100 long time St. Helena residents of our generation asking for favorite recipes from the years they were raising their families.

You will see there are many similarities. Because this is a community memoir, I was interested in discovering trends and have included the similar recipes. Anne Cutting and Mary Novak were across the street neighbors. Each of them contributed slightly different quick supper fixes using Dennison's chili and Frito corn chips

When I was married in 1962, Peg Bracken's, *The I Hate to Cook Book* was a popular shower gift and became a kitchen Bible for many. The simple tasty recipes "cut hours off" kitchen time by using canned soups and eliminating steps like browning, etc. Sunset Magazine tempted us with innovative California seasonal meal ideas, as well as bringing recipes from around the world to our tables.

Though many of us were not officially in the work place, we were occupied helping husbands in their efforts – either working at home or in businesses or wineries. These were the growing years for the wine industry and we all often had guests. We also needed economical, easy to prepare company food.

It's not that we disliked cooking, but often we couldn't get to the kitchen until 5:30. Simpler, quicker cooking was necessary.

summer suppers

During crush, 100° heat, frantic days at work, preparing dinner for family and visitors was taxing. One had a quick swim and after cooling off, a garden visit to harvest for supper. Usually because of the heat, I prepared a main dish in the morning to serve cold.

Holidays were an exception. All the old family traditional dishes were on the table. There were Christmas cookie exchanges, holiday brunch, lunch, cocktail and dinner gatherings. Clubs, businesses and service groups had holiday parties – many were potlucks.

remember Sip and Sample

While walking one or another of us has a "remember this" or "remember when" story – wine cake bake sales for town benefits, the Sip and Sample fund raiser. Oh, remember, all the work it was, but the food was great. Sip and Sample was started in 1968 by the High School Parents Club and continued until the early eighties. Held in early fall, in later years at Meadowood, it was a feast of hors d'ouveres made by parents and a glorious tasting of donated wines. In 1980 over 600 attended. That year St. Helena High School students assembled a collection of Sip and Sample recipes that is still popular today.

Walking through St. Helena neighborhoods, seeing familiar houses triggers memories and stories about those who'd lived there. Sylvia, Seana and Valerie seem to know everyone in town.

summer kitchens

Questions were asked about the not quite two story houses seen about town. This style house was built in the early part of the last century. Instead of a basement, service areas were at ground level; front porches and main living spaces were up a flight of stairs. Down below was an area for wood storage or furnace, an oil tank, a work space, a laundry area, possibly a place for animals and a simple summer kitchen. Becasue of summer heat and no air conditioning cooking "below" made for cooler houses. Frequently when a new appliance was purchased, the old fridge or stove was put below and the area used for canning and early morning summer cooking. Large pots and other canning equipment were stored here and sometimes a beautiful array of canned tomatoes, tomato sauce, peaches, apricots, pears, etc. This would keep the main part of the house cooler. Several walkers do some canning, jam, jelly, pickle making and olive curing, but hardly to the extent of previous generations.

In 1969 we moved almost next door to Sylvia and Bob Pestoni soon after coming to St. Helena. There was a vacant lot and Mary Maggetti's brown shingle house between us. Mary was born in St. Helena in the late 1800's. Shelived half way up Spring Mountain Road when she was a young girl. She was a true Italian cook and shared cooking hints and St. Helena stories with us. It's difficult to imagine now, but Mary and friends would go by horse to Pope Valley for a dance and return the same day. They loved parties. A considerable number of Chinese lived here when she was a young. All those old rock walls were their handiwork. When a Chinese person died they were buried with copious quantities of special foods surrounding the grave. After the ceremonies Mary and friends would sneak over to the cemetery and feast on the goodies.

zucchini

The vacant lot between our houses belonged to Sylvia and Bob. They asked us to join them on a garden project. We weeded, shovelled and spaded. Bob Pestoni brought manure from the pig farm that required much effort to work into the ground. Mary supplied us with ideas and we learned to make pesto and ways to cook zucchini. You will find numerous recipes for zucchini here – we all were never without "too much zucchini."

Square dancing was popular in St. Helena. There were at least three groups in town that met at the Lodi Lane Farm Center. Our group had 40 couples. Before the dancing five couples at a time planed and prepared dinner. Oh, what meals – stews, barbeques and during crab season, a crab cioppino feed. Louis Martini would tell the story of the origin of cioppino. At one time his father was a fisherman in San Francisco and the Italian and Portuguese fishermen would gather for a pot luck or "stone soup" meal. Fishermen would go among the boats saying, "chip in, chip in" in thick accents.

No pizza recipes were submitted because pizza was not an every day food item until later. Pizza was a treat in our growing up years. One went to a pizza parlor with red and white table clothes, straw wrapped Chianti bottles holding candles and fake grape vines draped across the ceiling.

When Julia Child appeared on television she introduced us to more elaborate cooking, beginning a "revolution" in food preparation. In the early 1960's there were only a few restaurants in the Napa Valley. M.F.K. Fisher one of America's great food writers did live in St. Helena. A great interest in food blossomed as the wine industry grew throught the 1960's and 1970's. Many of these dishes disappeared from our tables. We are careful now with counting calories, eliminating fats and healthier eating. We do not eat many of these dishes on a regular basis. However, they are well remembered and still requested by our families for special occasions and the comfort foods of yesterday.

Though I have tried many of these recipes during the course of this project, I have not made any attempt to test them, trusting that they truly are tried and true. I have made no attempts to determine ingredient values, calories, etc.

Thanks to all who have helped in this effort and to all who have given recipes to include. It wouldn't have come about without help, information, ideas, and encouragement from friends. Thanks to Char Butcher for helping with initial typing. Beth Rodda and Tracy McBride solved Mac problems and guided me in setting up format. Oh, the wonders of Adobe's In Design. Peter Green supplied me with numerous old cookbooks to use in the collages and others with design ideas. Sylvia Pestoni and Harolyn Thompson provided answers for inevitable questions. Carolyn Pride, Paula Young and Valerie Presten patiently provided tedious proof-reading. Is it 1 cup Cheddar cheese, grated or 1 cup grated Cheddar cheese? Is chili spelled chili or chile (both are correct, but chili more common.) Carolynne Gamble's advice with planning and editing kept on the right track. Thank you to Skylark Images in Cotati for digital imaging and other needed assistance. Happily, my family hasn't minded the time this has taken.

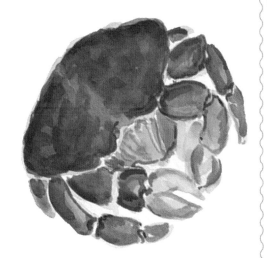

ST. HELENA'S WALKING WOMEN

Sylvia Pestoni
Sandy Herrick
Bev Popko
Jini Helm
Barbara Shurtz
Judie Rogers
Edy Sorenson
Sue Greene
Sydney Mensch
Seana MacGowan
Kay Philippakis
Valerie Presten
Phoebe Ellsworth
Toni Nichelini Irwin
Paula Young
Carolyn Pride
Missy Doran
Sarah Galbraith

Breakfast and Egg Dishes

AN EGG IS ALWAYS
AN ADVENTURE
THE NEXT ONE
MAY BE
DIFFERENT

Oscar Wilde

DUTCH BABIES

SUE CROSS, VERA HAMPTON, HELEN DAKE, KAREN DAHL, PAULA YOUNG

Popular breakfast treat. These are all slightly different.

DUTCH BABY
SUE CROSS

Make a few – they go fast.

5 tablespoons butter
3 eggs
1/2 cup milk
1/2 cup flour
1/2 teaspoon salt
2 tablespoons lemon juice

Preheat oven to 425°. Melt 5 tablespoons butter in an 11" x 13" glass baking dish. Beat eggs, milk, flour, salt and lemon juice with mixer or in blender until smooth. Add to melted butter and return to oven. Bake 25 minutes. Serve with lemon syrup, fresh berries, powdered sugar.

DUTCH BABY
GERMAN PANCAKE
VERA HAMPTON

6 tablespoons butter (melt in an 11" x 13"
glass baking dish) in oven. You need to
watch it carefully.
6 eggs
1 cup flour
1 cup milk
1/2 teaspoon salt

Pre-heat oven to 450°. Blend eggs, flour, milk and salt. Add to melted butter and bake. Check carefully after 10 - 15 minutes, it should rise quite a bit, then lower temp to 375°-400° and bake 10 minutes more. Check carefully, as every oven is different. Cut into pieces and top with maple syrup, or fresh strawberries with sifted powdered sugar.

HULDAH'S FINNISH PANCAKE (SUOMALAINEN PANNUKAKKU)
HELEN DAKE

I made this often for Sunday family breakfast. It is especially good with peaches and yogurt. My mother said the Finnish farmers would make this recipe with the milk from cows that had just calved. The milk had an odd taste, but tasted fine in this oven pancake.

4 eggs
4 tablespoons butter
1/4 cup honey
3/4 teaspoon salt
2½ cups milk
1 cup unsifted white flour

Preheat cast iron frying pan or an 11" x 13" glass baking dish in 425° oven. Beat eggs, honey, salt and milk. Add flour, beat until blended and smooth. Remove pan from oven, put in 4 table-spoons butter. As soon as it melts, pour batter into hot pan. Bake for about 25 minutes or until knife comes out clean. Serve immediately with fresh fruit, yogurt, and honey.

Eating in St. Helena

FRESH BERRY DUTCH BABY
KAREN DAHL

2 tablespoons unsalted butter
1/2 cup all purpose flour
1/2 cup milk
2 large eggs
pinch of salt
fresh raspberries, blueberries or strawberries
powdered sugar

Preheat oven to 475°. Put butter in a 10" oven-proof cast iron frying pan and heat until butter melts and is bubbling. Beat flour, milk, eggs and salt with wire whisk or hand-held mixer. Pour batter into hot frying pan and return to oven about 12 minutes until batter is puffy and golden brown. Slide puffy Dutch Baby onto serving plate. Drizzle with maple syrup, fresh berries and powdered sugar. Cut in half and serve immediately. Serves 2

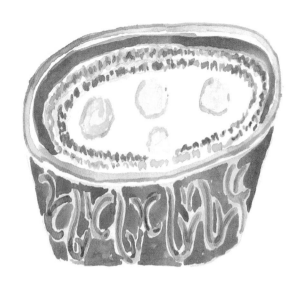

DUTCH BABIES
PAULA YOUNG

I grew up enjoying these. This is supposed to be a breakfast treat, but every once in a while, when Mom was tired, we had them for dinner, which made them even more wonderful. I now fix them for our grandchildren. They LOVE them. It is easy and fun.

1 cup flour
1 cup milk
pinch of salt
4 eggs
1 tablespoon sugar

Preheat oven to 425°. Mix flour and milk in a bowl, add eggs one at a time, beating after each addition with a wire whisk. PAM or lightly grease 4 individual oven-proof 1½ cup capacity dishes. Place 1 tablespoon butter in each and place in oven. When butter melts, add batter. Bake 25 minutes. Serve immediately with powdered sugar and a wedge of lemon.

BAKED EGGS
PHOEBE ELLSWORTH

For any meal. Easy to prepare. A save the day recipe when there's little in the fridge and no time to shop. Many possibilities.

BASIC INGREDIENTS
1 or 2 eggs per person
1/4 cup milk, cream or half and half per egg
salt
pepper

Preheat oven to 350°. Use buttered baking dish. Put milk in dish first. Gently break eggs into dish. Place baking dish in water bath and bake until yolks are well set and whites firm. About 30 minutes. Milk will set with egg whites.

ADDITIONS OR VARIATIONS
grated cheese
salsa - spoon a ring around edge
avacado slices
leftover or sautéed vegetables
chopped scallions
chopped or sliced tomatoes
artichoke bottoms or hearts
cooked sausage or bacon
cooked shell fish
herbs

CHILIES DE RELLENAR
FAMILIA DE ANTONIO MANZO

10 Poblano chilies
2 pounds dry cheese El Mexicano
13 eggs
15 Roma tomatoes
6 large Arbol chilies
3 cloves garlic
1 tablespoon oregano
2 tablespoons Knorr Suiza
2 teaspoons salt
5 cups vegetable oil
1 cup flour

Cook Arbol chilies with tomatoes. When cooked, blend in blender with garlic, oregano, Knorr Suiza and salt. Cut cheese into long slices and put on large plate. Wash Poblano chilies well and cut a medium-sized square in center of each. Remove all seeds inside with a spoon. Be careful as chilies will burn your hands. Put chilies on a griddle of medium heat to toast. Flip from one side to the other being careful not to burn them. If burned they rip. Remove from griddle to a cloth or plastic bag lined with paper towels so chilies sweat. Remove after 15 minutes and begin to carefully peel outer skin trying not to rip chilies. Insert slice of cheese and fill with tomato Arbol chili mixture. After filling, roll in flour. Begin to heat oil in large pot. Separate eggs and beat whites until stiff. Beat yolks with 2 tablespoons flour and fold in beaten egg whites. Dip chilies one by one in eggs and place in heated oil, spooning hot oil over the top. After both sides are well fried set them in a colander with something underneath to absorb draining oil. Let chilies rest 30 minutes. Heat salsa in a large pot and add as much water as you like. Add chilies, lower heat and let them simmer for 45 minutes. Serve with rice and beans.

POLLY'S GOLDEN EGG BAKE
BEV POPKO

When I was married in 1964, it seemed like every recipe called for a can of mushroom soup. My kids loved chicken baked in mushroom soup. That was the first thing they learned to cook. They are very fine cooks today so I will include a recipe from our son, Rick Popko (in hors d'oeuvres section) and a recipe I got from my mother-in-law that calls for a can of mushroom soup. I think it's the only recipe I still use that calls for mushroom soup. It's basically deviled eggs covered with mushroom soup. Don't laugh until you try it.

6 hard–boiled eggs, halved lengthwise
2 tablespoons mayonnaise
1 tablespoon minced onion
1 teaspoon prepared mustard
1 teaspoon vinegar
dash salt
SAUCE
1 can cream of mushroom soup
1/3 cup milk
3/4 teaspoon curry powder.

Devil the eggs and place in a greased baking dish. Mix soup, milk and curry powder and pour over eggs. Bake 350° 15-20 minutes.

CHILIES RELLENO CASSEROLE
SHIRLEY SPARKS

1 pound Monterey Jack cheese, grated
1 pound Longhorn cheese, grated
2 7-ounce cans whole green chilies
1 can evaporated milk
5 eggs
1 tablespoon flour

Mix cheeses together. Remove seeds from chilies. Layer chilies and cheese in casserole. Beat egg yolks, add milk. Beat egg whites until very stiff and fold into egg yolks and milk. Fold in flour and spread mixture on top of chilies and cheese. Bake 325° 60 minutes. Serve with salsa. Serves 8.

Eating in St. Helena

SPINACH SAUSAGE QUICHE
MISSY DORAN

1 9" frozen deep-dish pastry shell
8 ounces bulk pork sausage
1/4 cup chopped scallions
1 clove garlic, minced
1/2 10-ounce package frozen chopped spinach (about 5/8 cup)
1/2 cup herb-seasoned stuffing mix
1½ cups shredded Monterey Jack cheese
3 eggs, lightly beaten
1½ cups half and half
2 tablespoons grated Parmesan cheese
paprika

Preheat oven to 400°. Let frozen pastry shell stand at room temperature 10 minutes, do not prick shell. Bake 7 minutes. Remove from oven, set aside. Reduce oven temperature to 375°. Cook sausage, green onion and garlic in medium skillet and drain when done. Stir in spinach and stuffing mix. Sprinkle cheese first, then sausage mixture in pastry shell. Mix beaten egg with half and half and pour over sausage mixture. Bake 375° 30 minutes. Sprinkle with Parmesan cheese and paprika, bake 15 minutes more. Let stand 10 minutes before serving. Serves 6.

GREEK SPINACH PIE (SPINAKOPITTA)
SUSAN SMITH

7-8 cups spinach (best fresh or
4 10-ounce packages thawed-frozen)
1 medium onion, diced
2 cubes butter
6 large eggs
2 pounds ricotta
1/2 to 1 pound Feta cheese, crumbled
salt and pepper
1/2 pound filo dough, thawed

Preheat to oven 375°. Chop spinach and mix with diced onion. Melt 2 tablespoons butter in a large frying pan. Sauté onions until soft. Add spinach, turn up heat and cook until all moisture is gone. Remove from heat. Melt remaining butter in a small pan. Beat eggs and mix in cheeses. Add to spinach mixture. Season with salt and pepper. Carefully spread thawed filo dough out flat and cover with a moistened cloth so that the separate sheets don't become brittle. Butter a 9" x 13" baking pan and place a sheet of dough on bottom of pan. Brush lightly with melted butter and continue until you have a stack of 10. The dough sheets should be about the size of the pan, Spread spinach mixture evenly over on top and stack with another 10 sheets of dough, buttering them as before. Roll edges under so that it looks tidy. Bake 375° 15 minutes. Turn oven down to 350° bake 30 minutes more. If top layer begins to get too dark, cover with brown paper. Remove from oven and let rest 15 minutes before cutting.

SPINACH AND MUSHROOM FRITTATA
BARBARA STANTON

1 10-ounce package frozen spinach, thawed and squeezed to remove liquid
4 eggs
1 cup part skim milk Ricotta cheese
3/4 cup freshly grated Parmesan cheese
3/4 cup choppd Portobello mushrooms
1/2 cup chopped scallions, include tops
1/4 teaspoon dried Italian seasoning
salt and pepper to taste

Preheat to oven 375°. Whisk all ingredients together in a large bowl. Mix well. Oil a 9" pie pan and fill with mixture. Bake 30 minutes or until browned. Let cool 20 minutes, cut in wedges. Serves 6.

CORNED BEEF HASH
HELEN GHIRINGHELLI NELSON

My Dad prepared corned-beef hash after church on Sunday for the family during the winter months when the resort was closed. He would double the recipe and put a poached egg on top of each serving.

1 can corned beef
4 medium baking potatoes
1 large onion, minced
1/2 green pepper, minced
2 tablespoons butter

Bake potatoes in hot oven until they are just barely soft. In a skillet sauté onion and green pepper in butter. Add corned beef cut into pieces and sauté gently. Split potatoes, scooping out centers. Add to onions, pepper and corned beef, mixing well. Add a little cream if mixture seems too dry. Stuff back into potato shells. Serves 4.

TAHOE BRUNCH
SYLVIA PESTONI

This ideal, always popular, breakfast recipe came from the Pasadena Junior League cookbook.

12 slices sour dough French bread
1-3 tablespoons butter or margarine,
 softened
1 cup butter or margarine
1/2 pound fresh mushrooms
2 cups yellow onions, sliced
1½ pounds mild Italian sausage
1/2 to 1 pound Cheddar cheese, grated
5 eggs
2½ cups milk
3 teaspoons Dijon mustard
1 teaspoon dry mustard
1 teaspoon ground nutmeg
2 tablespoons finely chopped parsley

Remove bread crusts or leave them on for a crunchier casserole. Butter bread with softened butter and set aside. In a 10" to 12" skillet melt 1/2 cup butter and brown mushrooms and onions over medium heat 6 to 8 minutes or until tender. Season with salt and pepper and set aside. Cook sausage and cut into bite-sized pieces. In a 7" x 11" shallow casserole layer half of the bread, mushroom mixture, sausage and cheese. Repeat the layers, ending with cheese. In a medium-sized bowl beat eggs with milk, both mustards, nutmeg, 1 teaspoon salt and 1/4 teaspoon pepper. Pour over sausage and cheese casserole. Cover casserole and refrigerate over night. When ready to bake, sprinkle parsley over the top. Bake uncovered 350° 60 minutes or until bubbly. Serves 6.

GREAT BISCUITS
CAROLYN PRIDE

2 cups flour
5 tablespoons unsalted butter
1 tablespoon baking powder
1/4 teaspoon baking soda
1/2 teaspoon salt
2/3 cup buttermilk

Preheat oven to 450°. Cut butter into flour until crumbly. Add baking powder, baking soda and salt. Make a well in center and add buttermilk. Mix and then knead lightly in bowl. Pat out to 1/2" thick and cut into 9 biscuits. Bake 450° 11 to 12 minutes.

ANYTIME GRANOLA
DIANNE FRASER

8 cups old-fashioned rolled oats
1½ cups each firmly packed brown sugar
1½ cups toasted wheat germ
1/2 cup each unsweetened shredded coconut and unsalted, unroasted sunflower seeds
2 cups sesame seeds
1 cup slivered blanched almonds
1½ cups golden raisins
2 cups chopped dried apricots
1 cup chopped dried cranberries
1/2 cup salad oil
3/4 cup honey
1 tablespoon orange flavoring
1 tablespoon vanilla extract

In a large bowl, combine oats, sugar, wheat germ, coconut, sunflower seeds, almonds, apricots, and sesame seeds. Set aside. In a small pan, combine oil, honey, orange and vanilla flavors. Cook over medium heat, stirring, until bubbly; pour over oat mixture and stir to mix well. Lightly grease two 10" x 15" baking pans or two 11" x 13" glass baking dishes. Bake, uncovered, 325° 25 minutes until lightly browned, stirring occasionally. Mix in raisins and cranberries after baking. Will keep for up to a month in an airtight container at cool room temperature. Makes about 16 cups.

GOLDEN SPOONBREAD
SUSAN SMITH

For Valentine's Day, I serve this with lingon-berries and a dab of ricotta for a special breakfast. You can even cut out servings of spoon bread with a large heart-shaped cookie cutter.

2 cups milk
2 tablespoons butter
1 teaspoon sugar
1 teaspoon salt
2/3 cup polenta or yellow cornmeal
4 eggs separated

Put milk, butter, sugar and salt in a saucepan; bring to a boil. Add cornmeal, very gradually, stirring to prevent lumping, and cook over low heat, stirring constantly, for 3-5 minutes, or until thick. Remove from heat and let cool slightly. Stir in beaten egg yolks; beat egg whites until stiff and then fold into batter. Turn into a greased 1-quart square casserole dish. Bake 375° 30-35 minutes, or until firm enough for tester to come out clean. Serve from baking dish at once. Serves 4.

MEXICAN SPOONBREAD
SUSAN SMITH

1 16-ounce can cream-style corn
3/4 cup milk
1/3 cup salad oil
2 eggs, slightly beaten
1 cup cornmeal
1/2 teaspoon baking soda
1 teaspoon salt
1 4-ounce can California green chilies, seeded and chopped
1½ cups shredded Cheddar cheese

Mix all ingredients except chilies and cheese in order given above (wet ingredients first, then dry ones). Pour half of batter into a greased 9" x 9" inch pan or pie plate; sprinkle with green chilies and half the cheese. Spread remaining batter on top and sprinkle with remaining cheese. Bake 400° 45 minutes. Cool just enough to set a little before cutting into serving-size pieces. Serves 6-8.

CRANBERRY KUCHEN
LYNETTE BENSEN

This is a recipe my Mother made every Christmas morning while I was growing up. I have made it every year since. Now my kids are doing the same, if they are not here with us Christmas morning.

1 cup flour
1/2 cup milk
1/2 cup sugar
1 teaspoon baking powder
2 tablespoons oil
1 egg
1/2 teaspoon salt
3 cups finely chopped cranberries
TOPPING
2/3 cup flour
1/2 cup sugar
2 tablespoons butter

Beat flour, milk, baking powder, oil, egg and salt together. Pour into greased 8" x 8" pan. Cover with chopped cranberries. Mix topping to a crumble and put on top of cranberries. Bake 375° 30 minutes until lightly browned on top.
NOTE: You can use ½ cranberries and ½ grated apple. Recipe doubles easily - use a 9" x 13" pan.

BRAN MUFFINS
SUSAN SMITH

This is a recipe from Carolee Luper that we shared back in the days of living in the trailer on Spring Mountain. It's a tummy warmer.

6 cups bran flakes (from health food store)
2 cups boiling water
1 cup Wesson oil
3 cups brown sugar
4 eggs
1 quart buttermilk
5 cups flour
5 teaspoons soda
2 teaspoons salt

Preheat oven to 400°. Pour boiling water over flakes and let sit. Beat eggs. Mix eggs and sugar into oil and beat well. Add buttermilk. Sift four, soda and salt. Add milk mixture and flour mixture alternately to the bran flakes. This is enough for many mornings of bran muffins and lasts well in the refrigerator. When you are ready to cook them, you can add raisins, sesame seeds, walnuts, pecans or sunflower seeds, pineapple, apple bits or anything you want to the individual muffins in the tin after you've filled it halfway. Top off with more batter after adding something. Bake 400° 15-18 minutes.

GRANDMA LARSON'S COFFEE CAKE
DIANNE FRASER

I love this coffee cake. It was my mother's recipe. I used to make it frequently.

1 cup shortening
1½ cups sugar
3 eggs
1 cup milk
3 cups flour
3 teaspoons baking powder
1/2 teaspoon salt
1 teaspoon vanilla
FILLING
1 cup brown sugar
1 cup nuts, chopped
3 teaspoons cinnamon

Sift flour, baking powder and salt together. Cream shortening (we used to use half Crisco and half butter or margarine, but you can use all butter) and sugar. Add eggs. Alternate adding flour and milk to the mixture. Add vanilla. Spread half of batter into a greased and floured 9" x 13" pan, batter, then rest of batter and top with remaining filling. Pour 1/3 cup melted butter over top. Bake 350° degrees 45-60 minutes.

FRENCH BREAKFAST MUFFINS
VALERIE PRESTEN

Everyone in my family calls these French Breakfast Puffs. I first made them about 1969 for a family gathering. Ever since then, whenever we have a breakfast or brunch with my family, someone always asks for them. They're fluffy, buttery, reheat well, and are especially good when you butter them and sprinkle on more cinnamon and sugar before eating. I'm getting hungry already.

1/3 cup shortening
1/2 cup sugar
1 egg
1½ cups flour
1½ teaspoons baking powder
1/2 teaspoon salt
a bit more than 1/4 teaspoon nutmeg
1/2 cup milk
TOPPING
1/2 cup sugar
2 teaspoons cinnamon
1/2 cup butter or margarine, melted

Preheat oven to 350°. Grease 15 medium muffin cups (2¾" diameter). Mix shortening, 1/2 cup sugar and egg. Stir in flour, baking powder, salt and nutmeg alternately with milk. Fill muffin cups 2/3 full. Bake in preheated 350° 20-25 minutes. Mix 1/2 cup sugar and cinnamon. Immediately after baking, roll muffins in melted butter, then in cinnamon-sugar mixture. Serve hot. Makes 15 muffins.

Eating in St. Helena

PARKER TALBOT'S HOTCAKES
SUSAN EDELEN

We have Grandpa's hotcakes every Christmas. It is the tradition in our family.

4 rounded tablespoons flour
l level teaspoon baking soda
3/4 teaspoon salt
2 eggs
1 cup buttermilk

Sift flour, baking soda and salt. Beat 2 egg yolks, add 1 cup buttermilk and slowly add flour. Fold in stiffly beaten egg whites. Cook on griddle.

MALASADES (DOG EARS)
SYLVIA PESTONI

FROM HER MOTHER ALICE GUINZA

We loved these growing up and so did my children.

1 cake yeast, dissolved in ¼ cup warm water
1 ½ cups milk, scalded and cooled
4 cups flour
1/2 teaspoon salt
4 eggs
1/4 cup sugar

Stir cooled milk into dissolved yeast. Mix in flour and salt. Beat 4 eggs with sugar and add to yeast, milk and flour. Mix together and knead lightly. Cover and let rise 3 to 4 hours until at least double in size. Wet hands in milk and pick off small handfuls of dough and one at a time, pull into square shapes. Drop into hot oil and fry until golden brown. Drain and coat with sugar.

GRAMMA'S COFFEE CAKE
SYLVIA PESTONI FROM KAY MAHORNEY

1 cube margarine
1 cup flour
2 tablespoons cold milk
1 cube margarine
1 cup water
1 cup flour
3 eggs
1 teaspoon almond extract
FROSTING
1½ cups powdered sugar
2 teaspoons almond extract
milk
TOPPING
chopped nuts and maraschino cherries.

Cut margarine into flour until crumbly by hand or use food processor. Add milk and shape into a ball. Divide into two parts and roll each ball into a 3" x 12" inch strip and place on un-greased cookie sheet. Bring second cube of margarine, water and almond extract to a boil. Remove from heat, add flour, beat and add eggs one at a time. Spread this mixture onto the dough strips. Bake 350° 60 minutes. Frost while warm.

CRÈME BRULEE FRENCH TOAST
RUTHIE RYDMAN

This is a great Christmas treat. Some remove bread crusts, others use round French or baguettes with crust and others use challah. All are good – your choice.

1 cube unsalted butter
1 cup packed brown sugar
2 tablespoons corn syrup
1 8" to 9" round loaf bread
(or equal amount other style)
5 large eggs
1½ cups half and half
1 teaspoon vanilla
1 teaspoon Grand Marnier
1/4 teaspoon salt

Preheat oven to 350°. Melt butter with brown sugar and corn syrup in a small heavy saucepan over moderate heat, stirring, until smooth. Pour into a 9" x 13" x 2" baking dish. Cut 6 1" slices from center portion of bread. Trim crusts if desired. Arrange bread slices in one layer in baking dish, squeezing them slightly to fit. Whisk eggs, half and half, vanilla, Grand Marnier and salt in a bowl until combined. Pour evenly over bread. Chill bread mixture, covered, at least 8 hours and up to 1 day. Bring to room temperature. Bake uncovered, in middle of oven until puffed and edges are pale golden. Bake 350° 35-40 minutes. Serve immediately. Serves 6.

Breads and Hors D'Oeuvres

NET WT 8 OZ (227g)

BREAD

Is the

warmest

Kindest

OF ALL

WORDS

CAFE SIGN

SAUSAGE BREAD
MARJ DIXON

2 pounds sausage
2 frozen bread loaves
1 onion, chopped
1 clove garlic, chopped

Sauté sausage with onion and garlic. Let bread dough thaw and rise. When dough rises roll out and fill with sausage mixture. Roll up and bake at 350°.

CHEESE BREAD
LEONA AVES

1 large loaf sour dough French bread
1/2 pound butter
1/2 pound Velveeta cheese
1½ cups Best Foods mayonnaise
(no substitutions)
3 cloves garlic, minced

Combine butter, cheese, garlic and melt slowly in saucepan. When warm, add mayonnaise. Spread on split loaf of bread. Place under broiler and watch **CAREFULLY** as it cooks quickly and will burn.

PIZZA SPREAD
PAULA YOUNG

1 pound sharp Cheddar cheese, grated
1 medium onion, finely chopped
1 small can chopped olives
1/4 cup olive oil
1 clove garlic, finely chopped
2 pinches oregano
1 package English muffins

Combine ingredients and spread on English muffins. Bake 350° 15 minutes.

CRAB DIP
MISSY DORAN

1 can crab meat
8 ounce package cream cheese
1 tablespoon milk
1 teaspoon Worcestershire sauce
1 teaspoon lemon juice
2 tablespoons chopped green onions
Tabasco, to taste

Combine all ingredients and place in a buttered baking dish. Bake 350° 15-20 minutes.

SANDY'S SHRIMP DIP
RUTHIE RYDMAN

1 can shrimp soup
1 cup diced celery
1 cup mayonnaise
2 3-ounce packages cream cheese
1 bunch green onions, chopped
1 can shrimp, drained
1½ tablespoons Knox gelatin

Warm soup. Soften gelatin in 3 tablespoons cold water. Add to soup. Add remaining ingredients. Serve warm with assorted toasts and crackers.

A DIFFERENT GUACAMOLE
JUDIE ROGERS

This seemed so exotic and amazingly delicious in the late 50's when guacamole first became a popular appetizer here. It is still good.

2 large ripe avocados
1 teaspoon salt
3/4 teaspoon Tabasco
1/2 teaspoon Worcestershire sauce
4 tablespoons mayonaise
1 tablespoon chili sauce
2 tablespoons minced onion
2 tablespoons lemon or lime juice
dash vinegar

Mash avocados and set aside. Mix remaing ingredients together and add to mashed avocados.

ARTICHOKE DIP
DIANE LIVINGSTON

It goes so fast!

1 8-ounce can non-marinated artichokes
1 8-ounce package cream cheese
1½ cups grated Parmesan cheese
1¼ cups mayonnaise

Add all ingredients to Cuisinart and mix, leaving it a little chunky. Put in ovenproof baking dish. Bake 350° 20-30 minutes. Serve with crackers or toasts.

Eating in St. Helena

CHEESE SPREAD
CAROLYN PRIDE

This is a huge favorite with men and is especially good with drinks and watching football games. This recipe started (as far as I know) in Colusa County in the 1960's. It is still a "staple" in our family, 40 years later.

1 pint low fat dry cottage cheese
1 cup grated sharp Cheddar cheese
1½ tablespoons horseradish
2 green onions, minced, include tops or
equal amount of chopped chives
2 tablespoons mayonnaise
salt and pepper, to taste

Mix all ingredients together. Serve with Triscuits, Melba toasts or similar crackers.

CHEDDAR CURRY SPREAD
RUTHIE RYDMAN

2 cups grated Cheddar cheese
1 4½-ounce can black olives, drained and-chopped
1/2 teaspoon curry powder
2 green onions, finely chopped
1 clove garlic, minced

Combine all ingredients in bowl until well mixed. Refrigerate several hours to allow flavors to blend. Serve cold or at room temperature on crackers or sliced French bread.

BEER CHEESE DIP
BETSY HOLZHAUER

1 pound mild Cheddar cheese, grated
1 pound sharp Cheddar cheese, grated
1 6-ounce can tomato paste
1 teaspoon garlic salt
1 tablespoon Worcestershire sauce
1 12-ounce can beer

Mix all ingredients. Refrigerate several hours to let flavors blend. Serve with toasts or crackers.
NOTE: For variety with this or other dips use endive leaves instead of crackers.

CAVIAR PIE
SIENA O'CONNELL

This recipe came to Siena from her mother Blanche. No party was complete without it. Mary Beth Egner also used this recipe, which she got from Siena. It's always a Christmas Eve treat at Mary Beth's.

2 green onions, finely chopped
6 ounces cream cheese
l teaspoon lemon juice
dash of Worcestershire sauce
t tablespoon mayonaise
4-6 ounces caviar
2 hard boiled eggs, grated
lemon slices for decoration

Mash or use food processor to mix onions, cream cheese, lemon juice, Worcestershire and mayonaise. Spread out on a serving plate. Refrigerate until ready to serve. Just before serving spead caviar on top of mixture leaving a 1" rim around the outside for the grated egg. Garnish with lemon slices and serve with toasts or endive leaves.

HORS D'OEUVRES THROUGH THE DECADES
CONNIE AND GUY KAY

HOT SHRIMP CANAPES

In the 50's and 60's this was a favorite from the Nabisco Party Snacks Book.

1 5-ounce can shrimp
6 tablespoons mayonnaise
1/2 teaspoon salt
dash pepper
1/4 cup grated Cheddar cheese
Ritz crackers

Mash shrimp with fork. Add mayonnaise, salt and pepper. Mix well, spoon on crackers and top with grated cheese. Broil until cheese melts and is slightly brown.

GREENBRIAR PUREE DE FOI DE VOLAILLE (BRANDIED CHICKEN LIVERS)

In the 70's we had arrived in the wine country and this was a recipe of that era.

1 large onion, chopped
2 tablespoons butter
2/3 cup dry sherry
3 tablespoons brandy
1 pound chicken livers
1/4 cup chopped parsley
salt and pepper
endive leaves, Melba toasts, pumpernickel rounds or crostini

Sauté onion in butter until soft. Stir in chicken livers and sherry. Simmer uncovered 20 minutes. Place one half of mixture in blender and process until smooth. Remove to small bowl. Repeat with remaining half. Stir in brandy, salt and pepper. Cover and chill. Garnish with chopped parsley. Serve on endive, toast, rounds or crostini.

TORTILLAS WITH GREEN CHILIES AND PARMESAN

In the 80's and 90's we discovered the word, cholesterol, so new recipes appeared.

Sprinkle grated Parmesan on low fat tortillas and top with chopped green chilies. Broil until cheese is slightly brown. Cut into wedges with pizza knife.

CHERRY TOMATOES WITH SALT AND HERBS

*Very easy and great for summer time. Connie added the following words of wisdom from Sophia Loren. "There **is** a fountain of youth. It is your mind, your talents, the creativity you bring in your life and the lives of people you love."*

cherry tomatoes
Herbes de Provence
salt
Season tomatoes with salt and herbs. Place in a bowl and serve.

MEXICAN DIP
TERESE PARRIOTT

This makes a lot and is delicious. Make a day before using.

1 pound Monterey Jack cheese, shredded
2 tomatoes, diced
1 bunch green onions, finely chopped
1 small can diced green chilies
1 small can chopped black olives
1 bunch cilantro, chopped
1 package Good Season Italian dressing, prepared

Mix all ingredients together. Chill in refrigerator at least 2 hours. Good with tortilla chips or corn chips.

ZUCCHINI APPETIZERS
JUDIE ROGERS
(SIP AND SAMPLE- JANET THOMAS)

3 cups zucchini, grated
1 cup Bisquick
1/2 cup finely chopped onion
1/2 cup grated Parmesan cheese
2 tablespoons parsley, chopped
1/2 teaspoon salt
1/4 teaspoon marjoram or oregano
dash pepper
1 clove garlic, finely chopped
1/2 cup oil
4 eggs, slightly beaten

Preheat oven to 350°. Grease 9" x 13" oven proof pan. Mix all ingredients thoroughly. Pour into pan and bake until golden, about 25 minutes. Cut into 1" x 2" pieces and serve warm.

Eating in St. Helena

CANDIED WALNUTS
VALERIE PRESTEN

Tasty as an hors d'oeuvre or snack. Also, delicoius chopped and used in salads.

1 cup brown sugar
1/2 cup white sugar
2 tablespoons light Karo
1/4 cup canned milk
1 teaspoon cinnamon
1/4 teaspoon nutmeg
1 tablespoon butter
1 teaspoon vanilla
3 cups walnut halves

Mix sugars, Karo, milk together. Heat to soft ball stage (236 degrees.) Add butter and vanilla. Beat until creamy. Add walnut halves and toss well. Turn onto waxed paper. Separate and let dry. Store in tightly covered can. Also freezes well.

HOT RED PEPPER JELLY
SYLVIA PESTONI

Serve over cream cheese on crackers or endive.

2 sweet red peppers, seeds and veins removed, finely chopped
1 green bell pepper, seeds and veins removed, finely chopped
3 jalapeno chilies, seeds and veins removed, finely chopped (wear rubber gloves)
6 cups sugar
1½ cups apple cider vinegar
1/2 cup lemon juice
2 teaspoons salt
6 ounces liquid pectin (2 pouches Certo)

Combine red, green peppers and jalapeno chilies in a large saucepan. Add sugar, vinegar, lemon juice and salt. Stir to mix. Bring mixture to a hard boil, stirring constantly, making sure mixture continues to boil while you are stirring. Cook, stirring constantly, for 5 minutes. Add liquid pectin and continue to stir and boil for 1 minute. Remove pan from heat and pour mixture into hot, sterilized jars and seal. Jelly will keep for a year, stored in a cool, dry place. Regrigerate if opened. Makes 7 eight ounce jars.

TUNA TARTARE
RICK POPKO

1 pound sashimi-grade tuna
2 tablespoons minced shallots
2 tablespoons minced chives
2 tablespoons mayonnaise
1/2 teaspoon kosher salt
1/4 teaspoon white pepper
1/4 teaspoon Piment D'Espelette (expensive Spanish spice)
1 tablespoon capers
1 tablespoon olive oil
1 tablespoon lemon juice

Cut tuna into small squares and mix with other ingredients. Serve on crostini.

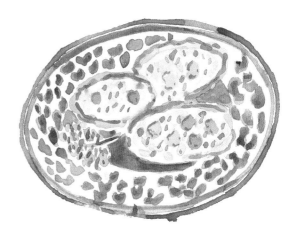

GREEN JALAPENO JELLY
SYLVIA PESTONI

Serve with red pepper jelly over cream cheese during the Christmas season.

3 medium green peppers, seeded and coarsely chopped
2 jalapeno chilies, seeded and coarsely chopped
1½ cups distilled white vinegar
6½ cups sugar
1 teaspoon cayenne pepper
6 ounces liquid pectin (2 pouches Certo)

Combine peppers in blender and puree. Add 1 cup vinegar and blend thoroughly. Transfer to a large, deep saucepan and add remaining vinegar, sugar and cayenne, blending well. Bring to full, rolling boil, stirring frequently. Stir in pectin and continue boiling 1 minute longer. Stir constantly. Remove from heat, skim off foam. Pour into hot sterilized jars and seal. Makes about 7 eight ounce jars.

Soups

SORREL SOUP
MARIANNE PETERSEN

4 cups French sorrel, stems, off
1 onion, finely chopped
1 cube butter
8 cups chicken broth
2 cups heavy cream
4 egg yolks

Sauté onion in butter. Add sorrel. When cooked, puree very fine. Add broth, cream and beaten egg yolks. Heat just to boiling. Serve hot or cold. Serves 12.

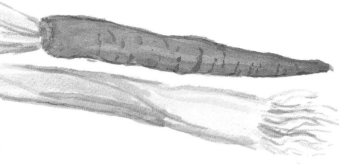

MINESTRONE
LOIS SWANSON

2 small leeks, washed thoroughly, white and light green parts, thinly sliced crosswise
2 medium carrots, peeled and cut into small dice
2 small onions, peeled and cut into small dice
2 medium celery stalks, trimmed and cut into small dice
8 new potatoes, halved or quartered
1 medium zucchini, trimmed and cut into small dice
3 cups spinach leaves, stemmed and chopped
1 28-ounce can whole tomatoes, drained and chopped
1 15-ounce can cannellini beans, drained and rinsed
1 Parmesan cheese rind, 2" x 5"
1 teaspoon salt
1 tablespoon fresh rosemary mixed with 1 teaspoon minced garlic and 1 tablespoon extra-virgin olive oil
ground black pepper
8 cups water

Bring vegetables, tomatoes, water, cheese rind and salt to boil in a soup kettle or pot. Reduce heat to medium-low, simmer, uncovered and stirring occasionally until vegetables are tender, but still hold their shape, about 1 hour. At this point you can finish preparation of soup or refrigerate in airtight container for 3 days or freeze for up to 2 months. To finish, defrost if frozen. Reheat and add beans, cook until just heated through, about 5 minutes. Stir in rosemary garlic mixture. Adjust seasonings, if necessary. Serve immediately.

SOPA DE GUADALAJARA
HOLZHAUER, NOVAK STAPLE
SUE CROSS

4 pounds boneless pork, 1 to 1½" cubes
1 onion, finely chopped
2 cloves garlic, finely chopped
2 teaspoons chili powder
1 teaspoon oregano
1 teaspoon cumin
7 cups water
2 cans beef broth
4 carrots, sliced
1 cup pinto beans, rinsed and drained

Brown pork in oil, add onion and garlic. Cook until onion is soft. Add water, broth, carrots and seasonings. Cook until meat is done. Cool and refrigerate over night. Skim off fat. Add pinto beans and reheat. Serve with cherry tomatoes, chopped green onions, cilantro, sour cream and lime wedges. Serve with tortillas.

SUSAN'S SOUP
SUSAN EDELEN

Great with French bread on a rainy day. I made this up.

2 cans Campbell's Bean with Bacon soup
2 soup cans water
1 soup can mild Victoria Green Taco Sauce
1 package Oscar Meyer center cut bacon, fried and crumbled
1 onion, chopped and sautéed
sharp Cheddar, grated, as much as you like
tomatoes, chopped, fresh, if in season

Mix everything together. Heat and enjoy.

Eating in St. Helena

GARLICKY BROTH WITH KALE AND SWEET POTATOES
BARBARA STANTON

This Tuscan-style soup brims with orange chunks of sweet potatoes and ruffled leaves of dark green kale, both of which contain certain potent antioxidants that help boost your immunity. The amount of garlic may seem like a lot, but it mellows with cooking. This soup freezes well.

3 teaspoons extra-virgin olive oil
1 large onion, diced
3½ teaspoons Italian herb seasoning
6 cups vegetable broth
2 15-ounce cans cannellini beans, drained and rinsed
1 pound sweet potatoes, scrubbed and diced
4 ounces kale, tough stems removed, chopped coarsely (about 4 cups)
12 medium garlic cloves, minced
salt and freshly ground black pepper

Heat oil in soup pot over medium heat. Add onion and herb seasoning and sauté until onion is soft about 6 minutes. Add broth, kale, potatoes, salt, pepper and garlic. Cook until potatoes are tender. Adjust seasonings, if necessary. Serves 6.

CHILLED GARDEN SOUP
NANCY GARDEN

1/4 cup olive oil
6 tablespoons Pepperidge Farm Dressing
2 cups tomato juice
1 bouillion cube in 1/2 cup hot water
4 stalks celery, finely chopped
1 cucumber, chopped
1 onion, grated
3 tomatoes, coarsely chopped
juice of 1 lemon
1/2 teaspoon A-1 Sauce
2 teaspoons chives, chopped
1/2 cucumber, thinly sliced

Combine oil and crumbs. Add tomato juice, broth, celery, onion, chopped cucumber and chives. Just before serving add lemon juice and A-1 Sauce. Pour in bowls, float thin cucumber slices on top. I love to add cilantro. Know your guests! Serves 4.

Eating in St. Helena

POTAGE BELIGIQUE
DIANNE FRASER

This is a favorite soup and I have made it many times. I use milk instead of cream.

4 tablespoons butter
5 large leeks, carefully washed and thinly sliced
1/2 pound mushrooms, thinly sliced
4 cups chicken stock
4 medium potatoes, peeled and sliced
I cup light cream or milk
salt and pepper to taste
fresh chives, chopped for garnish

Melt butter in a large saucepan. Sauté sliced leeks and mushrooms for 5 minutes, stirring constantly. Add chicken stock, salt and pepper and bring to a boil. Add potatoes and simmer, partially covered 30 minutes. Blend until smooth in blender or food processor, adding cream or milk. Garnish with chives. Serve hot or cold. To reheat, stir over low heat or in top of double boiler. Do not boil. Serves 10 to 12.

GRANDMOTHER'S POTATO SOUP
THERESA FREY

5 quarts water
2 cups flour
5 medium white potatoes, peeled, halved and sliced
1 leek, sliced
1 carrot, sliced
1/2 celery root, cut in 3 wedges
grated nutmeg
4 beef bouillon cubes
salt to taste

Roast flour in 5 quart pan. This is the trickiest part of the soup, as flour burns easily. If it does, discard and start over with a clean and dry pan. Heat should be medium. Stir with wooden ladle, shake and stir continuously, then change to wire whisk. No lumps are allowed. Slowly add water and let it simmer 45 minutes, stirring frequently. Then add vegetables, bouillon cubes and cook until potatoes are falling apart. You may have to add more water. This is a very hearty winter soup. It makes a meal. We used to cut up a smoked bratwurst in each soup bowl and of course, serve bread. As children we used to fight for a celery wedge. Still today!! It is just the best.

Vegetable Dishes

IF a MAN
REALLY
LIKES
POTATOES

HE MUST BE A
DECENT SORT
OF FELLOW

A.A.MILNE

COLLINS FAMILY MUSHROOMS
KATHY COLLINS

This smells great while cooking and disappears when served! Cooking time is correct.

4 pounds mushrooms, stems removed
2 cubes butter
1 bottle Napa Valley red wine
2 tablespoons Worcestershire sauce
1 teaspoon dill seed
1 teaspoon ground pepper
1 clove garlic, minced
2 cups beef or chicken stock
salt to taste

Combine all ingredients except salt in a large pot. Bring to boil slowly, reduce to simmer. Cook 5-6 hours covered, then another 3-5 hours uncovered until liquid barely covers mushrooms or almost all liquid is absorbed. Serve in warm chafing dish or as an accompaniment to meat. Serves about 12.

SWEET AND SOUR RED CABBAGE
PAULA YOUNG

1/2 head red cabbage
3 slices bacon, chopped
4 tablespoons white vinegar
3 tablespoons brown sugar
1/8 teaspoon pepper

Shred cabbage. Fry bacon. Remove from pan and add cabbage to drippings. Cook 5 minutes. Add vinegar, sugar, salt and pepper. Stir and cook 5 minutes more. Garnish with bacon.

CORN CASSEROLE
LINDA BERTOLI

Everyone will ask you for this recipe!

1 16-ounce can whole kernel corn, drained
1 16-ounce can creamed corn
1 cup sour cream
2 eggs, beaten
1 8-ounce package corn bread mix
1 small onion, grated
Cheddar cheese, grated

Preheat oven to 350°. Assemble all ingredients except cheese and place in a greased 8" x 8" glass baking dish. Top with grated cheese. Bake 45 minutes at 350°.

FRIED GREEN TOMATOES
JUDIE ROGERS

In the fall, as the weather cools and vine ripened tomatoes are past, there are still green tomatoes on the vine that can be used for green tomato pie, green tomato chutney or Fried Green Tomatoes.

sourdough pancake mix
very green tomatoes, sliced 1/4" to 1/3" thick
grapeseed oil.

Prepare batter. Heat oil until hot in a pan that conducts heat evenly. Lightly dip tomatoes in batter. Fry until brown, turning once. Drain on paper towels. Serve immediately with creamed horseradish (half sour cream, half horseradish.)

BUFFET VEGETABLES
CAROLYN PRIDE

1 small package frozen cut green beans
2 cups celery, sliced 1/2" pieces
2 cups carrots, sliced, 1/2" pieces
1 large onion. peeled, thick slices, separate rings
1 red or green bell pepper, cut into 1" squares
1 8-ounce can sliced water chestnuts
4 medium tomatoes, wedged, drained
6 tablespoons butter
DRY MIX
1 tablespoon tapioca
3/4 teaspoon seasoned salt
1 tablespoon sugar
1/2 to 3/4 teaspoon salt and 1½ teaspoon pepper

Mix vegetables in large bowl. Place half of vegetable mix in a 1 to 1½" flat baking dish. Sprinkle all of dry mix over vegetables and top with rest of vegetables. Dot with butter. Cover with foil. Bake 350° 45-50 minutes. Uncover. Bake 15-20 minutes more.

Eating in St. Helena

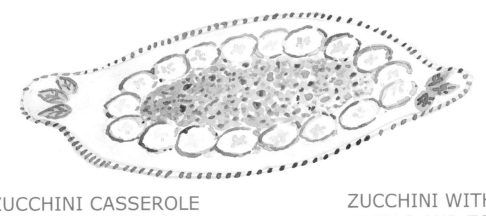

ZUCCHINI CASSEROLE
JOHN NYQUIST

I really dug back into old recipes for this one. It's so good and old-fashioned.

4 cups sliced zucchini, 1/2" thick
2 cups boiling water
2 eggs
1 cup mayonnaise
1 onion, chopped medium fine
1/4 cup chopped green pepper
salt and pepper to taste
1 cup grated Parmesan cheese
1 tablespoon butter
2 tablespoons buttered bread crumbs, soft

Cook zucchini in boiling water for 2 minutes. Drain well. In a large bowl beat eggs, stir in mayonnaise, onion, green pepper, cheese, salt and pepper to taste. Add zucchini. Turn into a buttered 1½ quart baking dish. Dot with butter, sprinkle with bread crumbs. Bake 350° 30 minutes. Serves 6.

SAVORY ZUCCHINI
PAULA YOUNG

4 zucchini, 9" to 10" long
8 slices bacon
1/4 teaspoon dry mustard
2 teaspoons sugar
1 tablespoon basil, chopped
2 tablespoons cider vinegar
1½ cups croutons
2 tablespoons olive oil.

Steam whole zucchini for 12 to 15 minutes until barely fork tender. Remove to buttered baking dish. Cut bacon into small pieces and cook in a skillet. Stir in mustard, sugar, basil and vinegar. Heat olive oil and sauté croutons until they have absorbed oil and are slightly brown. Add croutons to bacon mixture. Make a deep slit in each zucchini and fill with bacon, crouton mixture. Bake 20 minutes.

ZUCCHINI WITH SPLIT LENTILS AND TOMATOES
KATHY CARRICK

The nutty flavor of lentils goes particularly well with zucchini and tomatoes, perked up with a selection of aromatic spices. Serve with rice or bread for a filling and tasty supper. This recipe calls for "curry leaves". Kathy has scanned many on-line herb suppliers, including Indian specialty herb sites and they don't exist. She continues, saying that a friend at CIA says that curry is an herb that CIA has grown, but unless used fresh, becomes bitter. So she's stopped her quest and hopes the lack of curry leaves has no impact on the flavor.

8 ounces zucchini
1 large onion, finely sliced
2 cloves garlic, crushed
2 fresh green chilies, chopped
2/3 cup mung dhal or yellow split peas
1/2 teaspoon ground turmeric
1/4 cup vegetable oil
1/2 teaspoon mustard seeds
1/2 teaspoon cumin seeds
1/4 teaspoon asafetida
a few fresh cilantro and mint leaves, chopped
6-8 curry leaves (if available)
1/2 teaspoon granulated sugar
1 7-ounce can tomatoes, chopped or fresh tomatoes
1/4 cup lemon juice
salt

Cut zucchini into wedges, Finely slice onion and crush garlic. Chop green chilies. Simmer lentils and turmeric in 1¼ cups water until cooked but not mushy. Drain, retaining cooking liquid. Sauté zucchini, sliced onion, garlic and chilies. Add mustard and cumin seeds, asafetida, cilantro and mint and stir in curry leaves (*if available*) and sugar. Add tomatoes and salt. Cover and cook until zucchini is nearly tender, but still crunchy. Fold in drained lentils and lemon juice. If dish is too dry, add some of reserved cooking liquid. Reheat thoroughly and serve. Serves 4-6.

MEXICAN ZUCCHINI
CAROLYN PRIDE

2 tablespoons olive oil
4 cups thinly sliced zucchini
2/3 cup chopped celery
1/2 large onion, chopped
1/2 cup sliced red or green bell pepper
fresh basil, chopped, to taste
1/2 cup picante sauce, hot or mild, to taste
1 teaspoon salt
pepper, freshly ground, to taste
1 cup grated Monterey Jack cheese

Heat olive oil in large skillet. Sauté all vegetables together for 3 minutes, stirring constantly. Add basil, picante sauce, salt and pepper, stir well. Add Monterey Jack cheese and mix well. When cheese is barely melted, serve immediately.

ZUCCHINI PANCAKES
PHOEBE ELLSWORTH

My son, Geoff did not like zucchini. He would always catch me no matter how I tried to conceal zucchini. I tried putting zucchini in many dishes. The look on my face gave it away.

2 pounds raw zucchini, grated
1 cup flour
2 teaspoons baking powder
2 eggs, well beaten
salt, pepper
1/2 teaspoon thyme
1/2 butter - 1/2 olive oil, for frying

Put grated zucchini in bowl. Sift flour and baking powder and mix with zucchini. Beat in eggs and seasonings. Heat butter and olive oil mixture in frying pan. Drop spoonfuls of batter into frying pan turning when brown.

ZUCCHINI, PESTO, PASTA

One last quick, delicious zucchini recipe.

zucchini, julliened
1/2 pound noodles, cooked
1/2 cup pesto
Parmesan cheese, grated
toasted walnuts or pine nuts

Sauté zucchini in olive oil. Add cooked noodles and small amount of water or broth. Toss well and add pesto and nuts. Serve with grated Parmesan cheese.

BROCCOLI CASSEROLE
SUSAN EDELEN

1 box frozen chopped broccoli or
1 bunch fresh broccoli
1/2 can cream of mushroom soup
1 egg beaten
1/2 cup grated sharp Cheddar
1/2 cup mayonaise
1 tablespoon minced onion
salt and pepper

Cook broccoli only until crunchy, Drain well. Mix with soup, egg, cheese, mayonaise, onion, salt and pepper. Place in buttered casserole and dot with butter. Bake 350° 30 minutes. Serves 8. I always double the recipe because what are you going to do with half a can of soup.

STUFFED ARTICHOKES
BECKY PARRIOTT

4 medium artichokes
3 stacks soda crackers
1 onion, diced or grated
3 cloves garlic, diced
3/4 cup grated Parmesan cheese
1/2 teaspoon dry basil
1/2 teaspoon oregano
1 teaspoon salt or to taste
pepper, to taste
3/4 cups olive oil

Cut tops of artichokes so they are flat, then cut each leaf enough to remove stickers. Rinse and drain. In a food processer process garlic, add onion and process until fine. Place in a large bowl. Without cleaning processor, process one stack of soda crackers at a time and add to bowl. Add seasonings and mix well. Add cheese and olive oil, a little at a time. Mixture needs to be moist. Pull artichoke leaves apart and put cracker mixture inside leaves, working from bottom up, using your thumb to press stuffing down between leaves. Work toward center of artichoke as far as you can pull leaves apart. Put more stuffing on top of stuffing already in artichoke. Place in a large steamer with a lot of water. Bring to a boil, turn down to medium heat, cover and steam for 60-90 minutes. When done stuffing will be molded to the leaf. Check for doneness after 60 minutes - outer leaf should pull off easily.

Eating in St. Helena

EGGPLANT CRUNCH CASSEROLE
BECKY PARRIOTT

Coarsely crushed corn chips add crunch and enhance eggplant flavor.

1 pound eggplant, peeled and cubed
1 cup chopped celery
1/2 cup chopped onion
1/2 cup chopped green pepper
4 tablespoons butter
1 8-ounce can tomato sauce
4 ounces sharp American cheese, shredded
1½ cups coarsely chopped corn chips
OPTIONAL
1 pound ground beef, cooked and crumbled

In a large skillet or saucepan, cook egglant, celery, onion and green pepper in butter until tender, about 15 minutes. Stir in tomato sauce, cheese, meat, if used, and 1 cup corn chips. Turn into a 1½ quart casserole. Bake covered 350° 25 -30 minutes until heated through. Wreathe with remaining 1/2 cup corn chips before serving. Serves 6 to 8.

CAPONATA
RUTHIE RYDMAN AND PHOEBE ELLSWORTH

This recipe came from the San Francisco Junior League cookbook. Ruthie says she makes it all the time. I savor Caponata when tomatoes are ripe – a summer favorite. Caponata is an interesting variation of ratatouille. It keeps beautifully, travels well, and is best served at room temperature or only slightly warm.

1 cup olive oil
1½ pound eggplant, peeled and cut into 1 inch cubes
2 large green peppers, cut into 1 inch pieces
2 large onions, diced
2 cloves garlic, minced
1 28-ounce can solid pack tomatoes, drained or fresh tomatoes
1/3 cup red wine vinegar
2 tablespoons sugar
2 tablespoons capers
2 tablespoon tomato paste
2 teaspoons salt
1/2 cup chopped fresh parsley
1/2 cup pimento stuffed green olives, rinsed and thickly sliced
1/2 teaspoon freshly ground pepper
1 tablespoon or more chopped fresh basil or dried basil, crumbled
1/2 cup pine nuts, sautéed in olive oil

In a large, heavy saucepan combine olive oil, eggplant, green peppers, onions, garlic and tomatoes. Cook 20 to 30 minutes or until just tender. Add wine vinegar, sugar, capers, tomato paste, salt, parsley, green olives, pepper and basil. Cover and simmer 15 minutes. Add pine nuts and serve warm, not hot, at room temperature or cold. May be refrigerated up to 3 weeks. Serves 10-12.

COPPER PENNIES
BETSY HOLZHAUER

5 cups carrots, sliced and cooked until firm – 7-10 minutes
(approximately 10-12 carrots)
1 medium onion, chopped
1 green pepper, chopped
1 10¾ ounce can condensed tomato soup
1/2 cup oil
3/4 cup white rice vinegar
1 teaspoon salt
1 teaspoon dry mustard
1/2 teaspoon pepper
1 teaspoon Worcestershire sauce

Mix first 3 ingredients. Blend all other ingredients into a sauce. Pour sauce over vegetables. Place in covered jars. Refrigerate over night. Will keep in refrigerator for 2 weeks. Yields 3 pints.

Eating in St. Helena

ONION PIE
SALLY TANTAU

rich unbaked pie shell
2 cups thinly sliced onions
3 tablespoons butter
1/2 cup cream
1 beaten egg
salt, pepper and nutmeg
Parmesan cheese, grated

Sauté onions in butter until transparent. Place in pie shell. Make custard of cream and egg. Season with salt, pepper and nutmeg. Pour over onions and sprinkle generously with Parmesan cheese and dash of paprika. Bake 350° 30 minutes.

POMMES ANNA
SCALLOPED POTATOES
VIRGINIA RAYMOND

Coming from a beef and potato family, we have enjoyed this dish for years. It really makes a meal special and goes well with any of the Raymond dinners with Raymond wines. My mother-in-law, Martha Jane Raymond, used to make a similar potato casserole in the 50's, 60's and 70's using American cheese, sliced onions, flour and whole milk. This was a favorite of her children. Potatoes Anna are simply sublime and go great with a special dinner of any roast beef, roast lamb or chicken.

2½ cups whipping cream
1 tablespoon butter
2 cloves garlic
5 large all purpose potatoes
1/4 cup freshly grated Parmesan cheese
salt and pepper

Simmer cream, butter and garlic in a small sauce pan for 15 minutes or until cream has reduced to half of original quantity. Slice potatoes thinly and dry on paper towels. Butter a small casserole and arrange potatoes in even layers. Sprinkle a little Parmesan, salt and pepper on each layer. Cover potatoes with reduced cream, adding additional cream, if necessary, to cover potatoes completely. Cover. Bake 350° 90 minutes. Lid can be removed last 15-20 minutes to brown slightly. Serves 6.

CATHY CAMPBELLS
POTATO CASSEROLE
RUTHIE RYDMAN

Boys love this dish.

6 medium potatoes, peeled, cooked and shredded
1 pint sour cream
¼ cup butter
1 can cream of celery soup
1/3 cup chopped green onions
1½ cups grated Cheddar cheese
1 cup cornflakes, crushed in 2 tablespoons melted butter

Heat butter and soup. Add onion and cheese. Fold in sour cream. Place potatoes in ovenproof baking dish. Cover with soup mixture and top with corn flakes. Bake 350° 45 minutes.

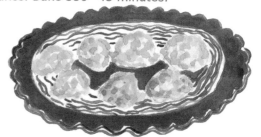

HUSH PUPPIES
SEANA MCGOWAN

2 cups cornmeal
1 tablespoon flour
1/2 teaspoon baking soda
1 teaspoon baking powder
1 teaspoon salt
1 egg
3 tablespoons finely chopped onion
1 cup buttermilk

Mix all dry ingredients together. Add onions, milk and beaten egg. Drop by spoonfuls into pan or kettle of hot oil. Fry to golden brown. If a deep kettle is used hush puppies will come to top when done.

RICE PILAU
SUSAN EDELEN from MARIAN T. HALL

My mother served this as a side dish with leg of lamb on Sundays with we four children being, for once, on our best behavior.

Sauté one chopped yellow onion in butter. Add 1 cup uncooked Uncle Ben's rice and 2 cups water, laced with 8 dissolved chicken bouillon cubes. Place in covered baking dish. Bake 375° 30 minutes. Stir in 2 tablespoons butter before serving.

Eating in St. Helena

CELERY ROOT
AND SWEET POTATO MASH
DIANA STOCKTON

Although my children have all become excellent cooks, I am still struggling in my father's shadow. He was the inspired cook of my childhood who taught me many arts of housewifery and husbandry: how to wash dishes and set a tray: how to make a perfect roast beef sandwich and one of sardines: how to knit, roll a cigarette and drink Martinis. His favorite vegetables included Brussels sprouts and celery root. I married into a family that also liked Brussels sprouts, so I've been able to cook them just fine for decades. It was the celery root that took me much longer to figure out, but I really like this vegetable dish.

**celery root
yellow sweet potato
salt, pepper, butter (all optional)**

Allow one third of a sweet potato per person and the same amount of celery root. Use yellow sweet potatoes not orange yams. Put celery root in boiling water with a bit of salt, if you wish. Cook root until it begins to soften. Peel potato, cut it into medium pieces and add to celery root. Cook together until tender. Drain, reserving a bit of water. Mash really well. Add some of reserved water, if mash seems dry. I serve it as is. You might wish to add more salt, pepper and butter - all a matter of taste and diet.

CRANBERRY RAISIN STUFFING
SYD MENSCH

**1/2 cup butter
8 cups bread cubes
1 cup chopped onion
1 cup chopped celery
1 cup apple chopped
1 cup cranberries
1 cup raisins
2 teaspoons sage
1 teaspoon thyme
1 teaspoon allspice
3/4 cup chicken broth**

Melt 1/4 cup of the butter. Add bread. Cook until lightly toasted. Set aside. Melt remaining butter, add onion, celery and apple. Cook 2 minutes. Add cranberries, raisins, seasonings and broth. Cook until cranberries begin to pop. Mix with bread cubes. Use to stuff bird or bake in covered casserole. 350° 25 minutes.

VEGETABLE BEAN STEW
KAREN DAHL

**1 red bell pepper, sliced
1 onion, sliced
1 teaspoon ground coriander
1/2 teaspoon cinnamon
1 can garbanzo beans, drained
2 large tomatoes, chopped or canned diced tomatoes
1/4 cup water
1 tablespoon lemon juice
1 teaspoon saffron
2 yams or sweet potatoes, peeled and chopped into 1" cubes
1 zucchini, sliced**

Sauté pepper, onion, coriander and cinnamon a few minutes. Add garbanzos, tomatoes, water, lemon juice, saffron and yams or sweet potatoes. Simmer 15 minutes. Add zucchini. Cook until tender. Serve with couscous and topping of
**1/4 cup olive oil
1 teaspoon cayenne pepper
1½ teaspoons cumin
garlic clove, minced**

THE GREEN BEAN RECIPE

Many said we must include this long time favorite.

**2 9-ounce packages frozen green beans
3/4 cup milk
1 can cream of mushroom soup
salt and pepper
TOPPING
2/3 cup French's french fried onions**

Thaw beans. Mix beans, soup, milk, salt and pepper in 1½ quart casserole. Bake 350° until hot, about 30 minutes. Top with french fried onions and bake 5 minutes more or until onions are browned. Serves 6.

Salads

LET ONION ATOMS
LURK WITHIN THE BOWL
AND HALF SUSPECTED
ANIMATE
THE WHOLE
SYDNEY SMITH

Parsley
the jewel of herbs
both
in the pot and on the plate
ALBERT STOCKLI

THERE IS NO SUCH THING
AS A LITTLE
GARLIC
ARTHUR BAER

Phoebe Ellsworth

CANTALOUPE SALAD
ALICE JONES

1 medium cantaloupe, 2 cups pureed
2 packages lemon gelatin
1½ cups hot water
1/2 cup cold water
1 tablespoon plain gelatin
1/2 cup sugar
3 tablespoons grenadine syrup
1 lemon – grated peel
2 tablespoons lemon juice
GARNISH
sour cream

Peel and remove seeds from cantaloupe. Puree cantaloupe by running it quickly through a blender. Dissolve lemon gelatin, hot water and plain gelatin in cold water. Combine and cool slightly, add cantaloupe puree and remaining ingredients. Pour into 1 quart melon mold or 8 individual molds. If melon mold is used, turn out on a bed of endive or garnish with frosted grapes and chopped mint leaves. Garnish with sour cream.

FENNEL, ORANGE AND RED ONION SALAD
BARBARA SHURTZ

For most of our married life, I have made a salad every night. The more ingredients I can put in a salad the better I like it. Tomatoes, cucumbers, onions and avocados go with greens in the summer. Fruits and celery are good in the winter.

2 medium fennel bulbs
1/2 red onion
2 oranges
2 tablespoons balsamic vinegar
1/4 cup olive oil
3 tablespoons chopped parsley, chervil or arugula

Trim fennel bulbs, remove stalks and discolored pieces. Cut into 1/4" slices and set aside. Peel oranges, divide into sections and remove white pith. Set aside six sections and cut remainder in half and set aside. Cut onion into thin slices and set aside. Make a dressing combining juice of the 6 orange sections, olive oil and balsamic vinegar and chopped herbs. Combine all salad ingredients in a glass or ceramic bowl. Add dressing and let stand at room temperature for 30 minutes. Stir occasionally. Serve as is, or on a bed of lettuce. Serves 4 or 6.

CRANBERRY SALAD
DIANNE FRASER

This is a favorite holiday salad and even though it has Jell-O, the family would be disappointed if I didn't make it for Thanksgiving. It is crunchy and not too sweet.

2 packages raspberry or cherry Jell-O, or one of each
1 cup diced celery
1 14-ounce can crushed pineapple, well-drained
2 cups hot water
1 cup coarsely chopped walnuts or pecans,
1 pound package coarsley chopped fresh cranberries, use food processor or blender

Dissolve gelatin in hot water. Cool. Add all ingredients to gelatin mixture. Pour into mold. Chill for at least 2 hours. Salad will keep for several weeks in refrigerator. Great with turkey.
Serves 10-12.

LETTUCE, CUCUMBER, FRESH MINT AND FETA SALAD
CONNIE KAY

1 head butter lettuce
1/2 English cucumber, seeded and sliced
4-6 ounces Feta cheese
1 bunch mint, torn or cut up
DRESSING
Half lemon juice (Meyer lemons best) and half extra virgin olive oil

BROCCOLI SALAD
LEONA AVES

3 bunches broccoli, 2" slices
2 bunches red seedless grapes
3 bunches green onions, chopped
2 cups thinly sliced celery
3/4 cup sliced almonds, walnuts or any
other nuts, browned in butter
3 to 5 slices cooked bacon, crisp and
chopped

Mix broccoli, grapes, onions and celery. Add
dressing, bacon and nuts just before serving.
DRESSING
2 cups Best Foods mayonnaise
1 cup sugar
2 tablespoons apple cider vinegar

COLD RICE OR ORZO SALAD
RUTHIE RYDMAN

*This came from Junior League's San Francico A La
Carte and served at many Napa Valley Summer
parties. Instead of rice I use Orzo pasta.*

5 cups chicken broth
2 cups uncooked long grain white rice
3 6-ounce jars -oil -marinated artichoke
hearts
5 green onions, chopped
1 4-ounce jar pimiento-stuffed olives, sliced
(optional)
1 large green pepper, diced
3 large celery stalks, diced
1/4 cup chopped fresh parsley
reserved artichoke marinade
1 teaspoon curry powder
2 cups mayonaise
salt and frshly ground pepper to taste

Cook rice in broth, drain and cool. Drain artichokes, reserving marinade, chop. Add to rice
with onions, olives, green pepper, celery and
parsley. Combine reserved marinade withcurry,
mayonaise, salt and pepper. toss with rice and
mix throughly. Refrigerate until ready to serve.
IF USING ORZO
Cook 2 cups Orzo. Cool and proceed as above.

TOMATO, BASIL, BRIE SALAD
TWO WAYS
SYLVIA PESTONI

*This wonderful summer recipe from The Silver
Palate can be prepared two ways, either with
pasta or day old bread.*

4 ripe large tomatoes, peeled and cut into
1/4" cubes
1 pound Brie cheese, rind removed, torn into
irregular pieces
1 cup frsh basil leaves, cut into strips
3 cloves garlic, peeled and finely minced
1 cup plus 1 tablespoon best quality olive oil
2½ teaspoons salt
IF USING PASTA
1½ pounds linguine
Parmesan cheese, grated (optional)
IF USING BREAD
1 day old loaf sour French baguette, 1" cubes

Place tomatoes, Brie, basil, garlic, 1 cup olive oil,
1/2 teaspoon salt and pepper in a large serving
bowl. Prepare at least 2 hours beofre serving and
set aside, covered at room temperature.
FOR PASTA HOT OR COLD
Cook linguine in 6 quarts water with 1 tablespoon
olive oil and 2 teaspoons salt 8 to 10 minutes
until tender, but still firm. Drain pasta and immediately toss with tomato sauce. Serve at once as a
war salad. Pass peppermill and grated Parmesan.
Serves 4 to 6.
FOR BREAD SALAD
Toast bread cubes in 350° oven about 15 minutes
until lightly browned. Turn to avoid burning. Cool
and mix into tomato mixture 10 minutes before
serving.

CHICKEN SALAD
SYLVIA PESTONI

A summer time staple. the possibilities are infinite. Brillat Savarin said, "Poultry is for the cook what canvas is for the painter." Macadamia nuts add surprise and crunch to this easily made version.

**4 cups roasted or poached chicken, 1/2"
pieces
1 bunch scallions, chopped
4 stalks celery, fine dice
2 cups red grapes
1/4 cup chopped parsley
1 cup macadamia nuts
curry powder to taste (mix with mayonaise)
1½ to 2 cups mayonaise
salt
pepper**

Mix above ingredients and serve on decorated platter.

SUMMER SUPPER
CHICKEN SALAD
PHOEBE ELLSWORTH

**2 tablespoons unflavored gelatin
1/2 cup cold water
1/2 cup chicken broth, boiling
2 cups chicken broth, cold
1 tablespoon lemon juice
1 cup mayonnaise
2 cups diced cooked chicken
1 green pepper, diced
2 stalks celery, chopped
3 hard boiled eggs, sieved
1/2 cup chopped parsley
1/2 teaspoon salt**

Soften gelatin in 1/2 cup cold water, 5 minutes. Add 1/2 cup boiling chicken broth and stir until gelatin is dissolved. Mix mayonnaise, lemon juice and 2 cups cold broth together and stir into gelatin mixture. Mix chicken, pepper, celery, egg, parsley and salt. Add to gelatin mixture. Rinse a six-cup mold or bowl, shake out water. Pour in aspic, cover and refrigerate until set, about 3 hours. Unmold onto a platter and surround with lettuce leaves, sliced cucumbers and/or sliced tomatoes.

SUMMER VEGETABLE SALAD
SARAH GALBRAITH

A favorite from Gourmet Magazine.

**2 medium zucchini, ½" dice
4 medium tomatoes, peeled and 1/2" dice
(seed and squeeze out if juicy)
2 yellow bell peppers, 1/2" dice
4 cups coarsely chopped arugula, stemmed
1 tablespoon lemon zest
2 tablespoons fresh lemon juice
3 tablespoons extra-virgin olive oil
1½ teaspoons sea salt
pepper to taste
1/2 pound orzo**

Blanch zucchini briefly in salted boiling water. Drain and refresh under cold water. Drain well. Combine zucchini, tomatoes, peppers, arugula and lemon zest in large bowl. Refrigerate until cold. Shortly before serving cook orzo until al dente. Whie it is cooking combine lemon juice, olive oil, salt and pepper and add to vegetables. Drain orzo and toss with vegetables.

PARSLEY POTATO SALAD
DIANNE FRASER

I think I made this for every Jazz Choir potluck. All four girls were in Jazz Choir, so it was made often.

**2 pounds small red potatoes
1 large stalk celery, finely chopped
1 egg, hard-boiled
1 small clove garlic, minced or pressed
4 canned anchovy fillets
1 tablespoon Dijon mustard
1/2 teaspoon sugar
1/3 cup olive oil
3 tablespoons white wine vinegar
salt and pepper
3 green onions, including tops, finely
chopped
1/2 cup chopped parsley**

Cook potatoes. Drain and let cool. Peel, if desired and slice thinly into a bowl. Add celery. In a blender or food processor, whirl egg, garlic, anchovies, mustard, sugar, and vinegar until smooth. Season to taste with salt and pepper, then stir in onions. Pour dressing over potatoes and stir gently. Cover and refrigerate at least four hours or overnight. Serves 6 to 8.

Eating in St. Helena

IRENE'S POTATO SALAD
PHOEBE ELLSWORTH

Irene Mantua was our neighbor at Bodega Bay. She was a local native and well known for her cooking. I liked chatting with her and hearing Bodgea Bay stories. In today's cooking this tasty salad might be known as the HIGH C (cholesterol) salad. No numbers given for ingredients – mix what you wish.

red potatoes, cooked and cubed
crab, cooked and picked, copious amounts
hard-boiled eggs
parsley, chopped
Best Foods mayonnaise
salt, pepper

Fold mayonnaise into other ingredients. Salt and pepper to taste.

BACON DILL POTATO SALAD
TONI NICHELINI IRWIN

2 pounds red potatoes, boiled
1/2 pound bacon, fried crisp and crumbled
1/2 cup sour cream
1/2 cup mayonnaise
2 green onions, chopped
1½ teaspoons dill weed, fresh or dried
2 teaspoons Dijon mustard
1/2 teaspoon lemon juice
1½ teaspoons salt
pepper to taste

Dice cooked potatoes. Mix other ingredients (except bacon) and add to potatoes. For best results refrigerate overnight. Sprinkle with crumbled bacon just before serving. Easily doubled or tripled.

GERMAN POTATO SALAD
SALLY TANTAU

6 large potatoes
1/2 onion, chopped
3 stalks celery, chopped
salt, pepper
1/2 teaspoon celery seed
1/4 pound bacon, cook and chop, save fat
1 heaping tablespoon flour
1/2 cup water
1/2 cup cider vinegar
1 teaspoon sugar
2 tablespoons chopped parsley
2 eggs, hard-boiled and chopped

Cook potatoes with skins on. Cool and peel. Cut up in small pieces and add onion, celery, salt, pepper and celery seed. Cook bacon and drain. Add flour to fat, stir until smooth. Add water and vinegar and cook until smooth. Add 1 teaspoon sugar. Cool slightly, add to potatoes along with parsley and hard-boiled eggs. Serve warm or cold.

POTATO SALAD WITH PANCETTA
PHOEBE ELLSWORTH

2 pounds red potatoes, cooked and cubed, not peeled
6 green green onions, chopped
3 stalks celery, chopped,
1 green pepper, chopped
3 hard-boiled eggs, sliced
1/4 pound pancetta, cubed and cooked
1/2 cup chopped parsley
3/4 cup mayonnaise
3/4 cup sour cream
salt, pepper

Mix mayonnaise and sour cream. Fold into other ingredients. Salt and pepper to taste.

Seafood

FISH
TO TASTE RIGHT
MUST
SWIM THREE TIMES
in
WATER
and in
in
Butter WINE

a polish proverb

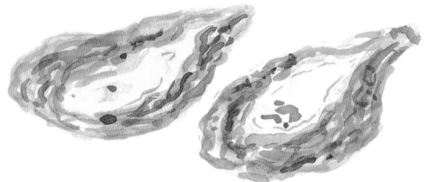

BAKED OYSTERS
HAROLYN THOMPSON

When I lived in the Pacific Northwest oysters were plentiful and inexpensive and I usually ignored them, until I had them baked (by my mother.) The recipe came to California with me in the '60's, and it was great to invite friends over on the weekend to roister with the oyster. While baking oysters makes them easier to open, oyster knives are still helpful.

PER PERSON
6-12 small or medium-size Pacific oysters, in their shells

Scrub shells well. Place oysters in shallow roasting pan, flat side up. Bake and serve in 2 to 3 batches
Bake preheated oven 400° 20 minutes (juicy)
– 30 minutes (drier, but easier to open)
Serve with hot melted butter, crusty French bread and a brisk Riesling. Begin with a tossed green

salad and finish with a fruit dessert.

SCALLOPS IN WINE
BARBARA RYAN

2 pounds scallops, well washed
2 cups white wine
1/4 cup butter
4 shallots, finely chopped
24 small mushrooms, sliced
2 tablespoons minced parsley
2 tablespoons flour
2-4 tablespoons whipping cream
1 cup breadcrumbs, browned in butter

Simmer scallops in wine. Drain and reserve liquid. Melt butter and sauté shallots, mushrooms and parsley. Stir in flour and blend well. Add reserved liquid and whipping cream. Add scallops to hot sauce. Place in shallow casserole and cover with browned breadcrumbs and place under broiler until golden.
8.Place under broiler until cheese is bubbly and fish is flaky.

BOUILLABAISSE
SEANA MCGOWAN

1 pound medium shrimp
1 pound scallops
1 large piece red snapper
 (or other firm fish), thick sliced
1 can minced clams
2 28-ounce cans tomatoes
1 can French green beans
1 cup medium dry sherry
2 large onions, chopped
2 cloves garlic, chopped
1/2 cube butter
1 pound mushrooms, sliced
1 cup grated Parmesan or Romano cheese
1/2 cup chopped parsley
1 bay leaf
1 can beer
1 teaspoon Old Bay seasoning
salt to taste

Boil shrimp in 1½ quarts boiling salted water and beer about 10 minutes. Remove shrimp and save broth. Clean, de vein and cut shrimp in half. Clean and slice mushrooms. Set both aside. Combine tomatoes, clams, sherry, parsley, some salt, juice from green beans, bay leaf and Bay seasoning in large pot. Cook slowly while preparing other ingredients. Brown onions and garlic in butter and add to soup pot. Bring shrimp broth to boil, add scallops, fish fillets, a little sherry and simmer 15 minutes. Add shrimp, green beans and mushrooms. Cook 5 minutes. Add this mixture to tomato mixture and cook until flavors mix. Serve with grated cheese. Fresh crab and/or oysters with juice can also be added. Serves 8.

42

MALAYSIAN CRAB
VALERIE PRESTEN

This basic recipe for Malaysian Crab came from a good friend who used to fly for World Airways. I have since refined it when cooking with a friend from Sydney, Australia and added a few of my own touches. This is a recipe you need to taste and make adjustments as you go, hence I've given no amounts for the ingredients. Don't be afraid to use lots of garlic and ginger; I've never used too much. I make it in a large wok and serve directly from the wok. Put it in the middle of the table with a couple of big spoons and let people dish out for themselves. With crusty bread and a green salad, lightly tossed with basic vinaigrette, it's a wonderful messy meal.

Sauté in oil (grape seed, olive, peanut, canola – pretty much any kind, but engine oil) lots of finely chopped garlic and freshly grated ginger. Stir in some chili sauce (bottled variety is fine), grated palm sugar (or white sugar,) maybe some catsup. Add lime juice and water. Cook gently a few minutes and taste. Adjust seasonings. Stir in cooked, cleaned crab that has been broken into pieces and cook for 5 minutes more. I've also added other shellfish, such as clams, mussels, scallops.

CRAB VICTORIA SANDWICH
SANDY HERRICK

A favorite of ours is a sandwich that the Ingomar Club in Eureka served. I'm sure there are many recipes for crab sandwiches and they are probably almost all the same, but we love this one.

FOR EACH SANDWICH
French bread, sliced
crab meat
mayonnaise
lemon juice, salt and pepper
Tabasco
cheese, Monterey Jack or Swiss, grated

Toast bread. Mix mayonnaise, crab, lemon juice, salt, pepper and Tabasco. Spread on toast, top with grated cheese. Bake at 400° until cheese bubbles.

Eating in St. Helena

SQUARE DANCE CIOPPINO
KATHLEEN PATTERSON

A St. Helena favorite. Use plenty of crab.

1 cup olive oil
2 large onions
1 large bunch Italian parsley
2 large cloves garlic
2 large cans solid pack tomatoes with juice
2 6-ounce cans tomato sauce
2 bay leaves
1 teaspoon oregano, fresh or dried
salt, coarsly ground pepper
2 cups dry white wine
1 pound medium shrimp, cooked, shelled, deveined
2 pounds bass, rock cod, halibut or other firm fish, uncooked, skinned, boned and cut into bite sized pieces
3 or 4 crabs, cooked

Heat oil slowly in a large, deep, heavy kettle. Chop onion, parsley and garlic together until fine and sauté in oil until golden. Add tomatoes, tomato sauce, bay leaves, oregano, salt and pepper to taste. Cover and simmer 1 hour. Add wine, shrimp and fish. Cook 10 minutes, stirring occassionally. Break up crab and add, correct seasoning and cook another 10 minutes. Serves 6 to 10 depending on appetites.

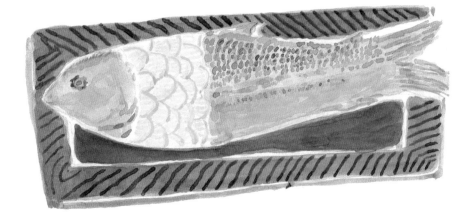

FARM HOUSE WILD SALMON
MIKE CHELINI

Willinda McCrea contributed Stony Hill Winery's winemaker Mike Chellini's recipe for his famous wild salmon dinner.

2 1 pound salmon fillets, 1" thick in center
1 tablespoon butter
1 tablespoon olive oil
1/4 cup flour
Kosher sea salt and freshly ground pepper

Preheat oven to 325°. Heat a non-stick frying pan over medium heat, add butter and oil. Lightly pat salt and pepper onto salmon fillets and coat them with flour. Shake off any excess. As butter begins to sizzle, but before it smokes, add fillets to pan skin side down. Cook fillets 2 minutes on one side until they become crispy and lightly browned. Turn over and brown second side for 1 or 2 minutes. Turn over so skin side is down. Place pan in oven for several minutes or until fish reaches desired doneness.

SAUCE
1 shallot, finely chopped
1/4 cup White Verjus*
or 1/4 cup lemon juice
1/3 cup Stony Hill Chardonnay
1 cube unsalted butter
* wine friendly vinegar substitute available at gourmet shops

Add shallot, Verjus and Chardonnay to a non-reactive sauce pan. Reduce over medium heat until almost all liquid has evaporated. Do not allow shallots to brown. Turn off heat and whisk in 1/2 cube butter. Over low heat whisk in remaining 1/2 cube butter, 1/4 cube at a time. Do not let sauce boil. Add salt and pepper to taste. Can be kept warm in double boiler for 20 minutes.

FRESH GRILLED WILD SALMON
PHOEBE ELLSWORTH

St. Helenans used to enjoy frequent summer meals of fresh wild salmon - broiled, baked, grilled or poached. "Those were the days." Now, limits on local salmon fishing and high prices of wild salmon from Northern waters make this a rare and special treat. Grilling a whole salmon was an adventure well worth undertaking.

7 to 8 pound fresh salmon
sliced lemon
sliced onion
dill

Fill cavity with several slices of onion and lemon and sprigs of dill. Wrap carefully in aluminum foil. Grill, checking freqently for doneness. Unwrap and serve with a lemon or sauce of your choice. Summer's finest meals include sliced tomatoes, corn on the cob with peaches and blackberries for dessert.

FISH FILLETS SUPERB
PAULA YOUNG

Yum!

2 pounds rockfish (I love snapper)
cooking oil
1 10¾ ounce can cream of mushroom soup
2 tablespoons sherry
1/2 teaspoon Worestershire sauce
1 tablespoon capers
1 cup grated cheddar cheese
paprika

Brush fish with oil and put under broiler 5 to 8 minutes - not too long as next step continues the cooking. Mix soup, Worcestershire and capers to make sauce. Transfer fish to heat resistant pan or platter. Spoon sauce over fish, sprinkle with grated cheese and top with a dash of paprika. Place under broiler until cheese is bubbly and fish is flaky.

Eating in St. Helena

PINEAPPLE SHRIMP
SARAH SIMPSON

1 pound large fresh shrimp
2 tablespoons flour
1 teaspoon salt
1 teaspoon soy sauce
2 tablespoons water
2 cups peanut or salad oil
1 cup water or pineapple syrup
4 slices pineapple
1/8 cup green onions, cut into 1½" pieces
1 tablespoon cornstarch
2 eggs
1 stalk celery, diced
2¼ tablespoons sugar

Make a paste of eggs, salt and flour. Clean shrimp by removing shell and black vein. Dip them in egg batter and fry in hot oil until they are light brown. Drain on unglazed paper. Cut each slice of pineapple into 8 wedge shape sections. Heat 1 tablespoon peanut oil in sauce pan, add pineapple, celery, water or pineapple syrup, soy sauce and sugar. When mixture begins to boil, add green onions, then thickening made of cornstarch and water. Pour over shrimp. Serve hot over rice. Serves 6.

JAMIE'S SHRIMP
IN NAPA CABBAGE WRAP
JAMIE DAIVES

J½ pound shrimp, chopped
1 egg white
1 teaspoon cornstarch
1 teaspoon sesame oil
2 tablespoons smoked ham, chopped
½ cup water chestnuts, chopped
½ cup Chinese mushrooms, chopped
½ inch fresh ginger, minced
2 scallions, chopped
1 tablespoon wine
1 tablespoon oyster sauce
½ teaspoon each - salt, pepper, sugar
1 teaspoon sesame oil
small amount water - cornstarch mix
4-6 Napa cabbage cups

Mix shrimp with egg white, cornstarch and sesame oil. Heat wok with a little oil and stir fry shrimp until pink. Remove to plate and add smoked ham. Add 1 tablespoon oil to wok and stir fry water chestnuts, Chinese mushrooms, ginger and scallions. Return shrimp mixture to wok. Add sauce made from cornstarch-water, wine, oyster sauce, seasonings and sesame oil. Cook until well blended and heated through. Serve in bowl with platter of cabbage cups to spoon mixture in.

SHRIMP CURRY
PHOEBE ELLSWORTH

Festive buffet dish. Ingredients can be varied.

vegetable oil
1 onion, diced
4 cloves garlic, minced
2 stalks celery
1 green pepper, chopped
3 or more teaspoons curry powder
1 teaspoon ground coriander
1/2 teaspoon ground cumin
1/2 taspoon salt
4 medium tomatoes, peeled and chopped
3 tablspoons flour
1½ pounds medium shrimp, peeled and deveined
1 cup water
1 cup frozen peas
1 13½ can coconut milk

Sauté onion, garlic, celery, green pepper in oil until tender. Add flour, stir and cook 1 to 2 minutes. Add curry powder, coriander, cumin and salt. Stir and add water. Add tomatoes and bring to a boil. Reduce heat and cook about 5 minutes. Add coconut milk and cook about 5 minutes. more Add shrimp and peas and cook for 2 to 3 minutes until shrimp are done. Serve over rice with condiment selection.

CONDIMENTS
chopped hard boiled eggs
chopped crisp cooked bacon
choppd peanuts
chutney
shredded coconut
chopped scallions
chopped cilantro

Main Dishes

HOW DO THEY TASTE? THEY TASTE LIKE MORE!

H L MENCKEN

DAD'S CHICKEN
SUE FOGARTY

One of Jim's favorites

1½ cups Minute rice
1½ cups coarsely chopped green pepper
3/4 cup thinly sliced onion
3 tablespoons vegetable oil
1/4 cup cornstarch
2 cups chicken broth
3 tablespoons soy sauce
2 cups chicken, cooked and slivered
3 ripe tomatoes, cut in wedges

Cook rice as directed on package. Keep warm. Sauté peppers and onions in heated oil in covered skillet over low heat until tender, but not browned. Blend cornstarch, broth and soy. Gently stir chicken and liquid mixture into cooked vegetables. Cook until sauce is clear and thickened. Add tomatoes and cook until just heated. Serve over rice. Serves 4-6.

CHICKEN LUAU
ANNE CUTTING

I have never seen this recipe in writing. Whenever we went to visit Cecil's parents in Hawaii his mother would make Chicken Luau. She was the original short order cook and this is so easy, but very yummy. I made it many times in St. Helena.

12 chicken thighs
2 packages frozen spinach – thawed and drained
1 can frozen concentrated coconut milk or canned coconut milk
salt and pepper
*optional – curry powder

Place chicken in a heavy casserole with lid. Cover with spinach and pour coconut milk over the works. Bake 350° 60 minutes. Serve over rice.

BETTY'S COMPANY CASSEROLE
BETTY BECKSTOFFER

Whether at home or with the family or going to a potluck at square dance, casseroles were always a big hit and we still love them today.

8 chicken tenderloins, cooked
1 bag or box of Pepperidge Farms seasoned stuffing mix
1 big sweet onion, diced
1 cup sliced mushrooms
1 cube butter
bunch of broccoli crowns, cooked al dente
prosciutto
Béchamel sauce with Gruyere cheese
chicken broth

Sauté chopped sweet onion and mushrooms in 2 tablespoons olive oil and cube of butter until onions are slightly opaque. Add stuffing mix and chicken broth (enough to moisten.) Salt and pepper to taste. Place mixture in bottom of casserole dish, layer cooked chicken tenderloins mixed with cooked broccoli with thin pieces of prosciutto and top with Béchamel Gruyere cheese sauce. Add additional 1/2 cup of broth or white wine. Bake 350° 45 minutes or until bubbling. Serves 8, but can be increased to serve many.

Eating in St. Helena

MARINATED BONELESS CHICKEN
DIANE LIVINGSTON

Marinate at least 48 hours prior to cooking. Left-overs are great for sandwiches.

10 chicken breast halves, boned and skinned
2 garlic cloves, minced
1/2 cup safflower oil
1/3 cup honey
1/3 cup soy sauce
1/3 cup Scotch whisky
3/4 teaspoon each, salt and pepper
2 large lemons, squeezed and sliced into chunks

Mix ingredients and pour over chicken and lemons. Marinate 48 hours. Grill chicken, it will be moist and delicious.

CALIFORNIA CHICKEN
SIENA O'CONNELL

This is still a favorite of all my kids. They request it on their birthdays. The recipe was contributed to "Easy Recipes of California Winemakers", by Mrs. Kenneth Dills whose husband worked at Charles Krug for many years.

3 chicken breasts, halved and boned
2 cups sour cream
1 10½-ounce can mushroom soup, undiluted
1/2 cup California Traminer or
Sauvignon Blanc
8 ounces Cheddar cheese, grated
1 3½-ounce can French fried onion rings

Place chicken breasts, skin side up in buttered baking dish. Mix together sour cream, mushroom soup and wine. Spread over chicken pieces. Sprinkle on grated cheese. Top with onion rings. Bake 350° 60 minutes. Serves 6.

CHICKEN AND ASPARAGUS CASSEROLE
SEANA MACGOWAN

2 chicken breasts, boned, skinned and cut into pieces (2" X 4")
1/4 teaspoon ground pepper
1/2 cup corn oil
12 spears fresh asparagus, cleaned, tough ends removed
1 can cream of chicken soup
1/2 cup mayonnaise
1 teaspoon lemon juice
1 teaspoon curry powder
1 cup grated sharp Cheddar cheese

Sprinkle chicken with pepper. Sauté chicken slowly in oil until white and opaque, about 6 minutes. Remove from pan, drain on paper towels. Line bottom of 9" x 9" x 2" baking pan with asparagus, cover with chicken. Mix together chicken soup, mayonnaise, lemon juice, and curry powder. Pour over chicken and asparagus. Sprinkle cheese over top. Cover with aluminum foil. Bake 375° 30 minutes or until done. Serves 4.

BARBEQUED CHICKEN
SANDRA PICKETT

An old-timer recipe I thought folks might enjoy. J.C.'s mother was using this when I first met the family in 1955. The recipe was old enough at that time and no one could recall where it had come from. We've been grilling chicken all across the U.S from West Virginia to Richmond, Virginia, to mid-central Ohio to Napa Valley for over 52 years. You won't believe this came out of the hills of Northern West Virginia (Morgantown) because it reads like California.

Melt butter and an equal amount dry sherry. Brush across chicken pieces as you grill them. Amount depends upon how much chicken you are grilling. I suppose modern day "HEALTHY" would be equal parts olive oil and butter.

LYDIA'S CHICKEN CASSEROLE
PAULA YOUNG

2 cups or more cooked chicken or turkey
1 cup sliced water chestnuts
1/2 cup slivered almonds
1 small pimento, diced
1 teaspoon celery seed
1 cup mayonnaise
2 tablespoons lemon juice
1 3½- ounce can French fried onion rings
1/4 cup (or more) grated Parmesan cheese

Mix mayonnaise and lemon juice. Place chicken in greased casserole dish. Sprinkle in water chestnuts, pimento, almonds and celery seeds. Mix mayonnaise and lemon juice and spread over top. Add onion rings and cheese. Bake 350° 30 minutes. Serves 6.

BALTI CHICKEN
KATHY CARRICK

This Indian chicken is great, takes less than 15 minutes to make. It is tasty and low fat. The use of yogurt, mint and cilantro give the sauce lots of flavor.

1 crisp green eating apple, peeled, cored and cut in small cubes
4 tablespoons cilantro leaves
2 tablespoons fresh mint leaves
1/2 cup plain low-fat yogurt
3 tablespoons ricotta cheese
2 fresh green chilies, seeded and chopped
1 bunch scallions, chopped
1 teaspoon salt
1 teaspoon sugar
1 teaspoon garlic, chopped
1 teaspoon grated fresh ginger
1 tablespoon oil
8 ounces chicken breast fillets, cubed
2 tablespoons golden raisins

Whirl the following in blender for 1 minute – apple, 3 tablespoons cilantro, mint, yogurt, ricotta, chilies, onions, salt, sugar, garlic and ginger. Heat oil in a wok or heavy pan, pour in yogurt mixture and cook over low heat for about 2 minutes. Add chicken pieces and blend together. Cook over medium to low heat 12-15 minutes until chicken is fully cooked. Stir in golden raisins and remaining cilantro. Serve over rice. Serves 4

CHICKEN BREASTS WITH MUSHROOMS AND FONTINA CHEESE
HAROLYN THOMPSON

This recipe has been a favorite for family dinners and for company for many years; partly because it's easy, partly because it's delicious.

4 half chicken breasts, boned and skinned
2 tablespoons butter or olive oil – or combination of the two
1 teaspoon nutmeg*
salt and fresh ground pepper
5 medium-large mushrooms, sliced
Fontina cheese – 1/8" slices to cover chicken

Pound chicken breasts to flatten a bit. Season with nutmeg, salt and pepper (can be refrigerated at this point for 1 to 5 hours.) Remove from refrigerator 15 minutes before cooking. Preheat oven to 400°. Heat 1 tablespoon oil in large skillet over medium heat. Sauté mushroom slices until lightly browned. Remove and reserve. Turn burner to medium high and add 1 tablespoon oil. Add chicken and brown about 4 minutes on each side. Place skillet in oven and bake about 10 minutes. Remove from oven briefly and place mushrooms on top of chicken breasts, then top with a slice or two of Fontina cheese. Return to oven for 5 minutes. (Check for doneness of meat.)
Serve with pilaf or boiled small red potatoes, asparagus or sliced avocado and sliced oranges. Serves 4.
•nutmeg is usually my first choice for seasoning, but cumin or crumbled basil are also good.

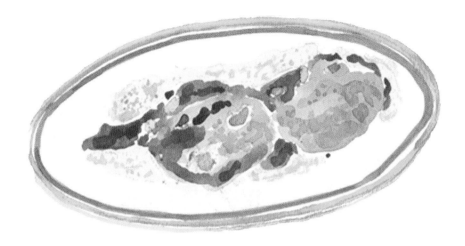

MEXICAN CHICKEN KIEV
TERESE PARRIOTT

8 half chicken breasts, skinless and boneless
1 7-ounce can whole green chilies
1/4 pound Monterey Jack cheese
1/2 cup fine dry bread crumbs
1/4 cup grated Parmesan cheese
1 teaspoon chili powder
1/2 teaspoon garlic salt
1/4 teaspoon ground cumin
1/4 teaspoon black pepper
6 tablespoons melted butter or margarine
SPICY TOMATO SAUCE
1 15-ounce can tomato sauce
1/2 tespoon ground cumin
1/3 cup chopped green onions
salt
pepper
liquid hot pepper seasoning

Pound chicken breasts between waxed paper until about 1/4" thick. Slit green chilies in half lengthwise and remove seeds and cut into 8 equal pieces. Cut cheese into fingers 1/2" thick by 1 1/2" long. Combine bread crumbs, Parmesean cheese, chili powder, garlic salt, cumin and pepper. Lay a piece of green chili and finger of Jack cheese on each chicken piece. Roll up to enclose filling, tuck ends under and secure with wooden toothpicks. Dip bundles in melted butter, drain briefly and roll in crumb mixture, coating evenly. Place bundles seam side down without sides touching in a greased 9" x 11" baking dish. Cover and chill at least 4 hours or overnight. To serve, uncover and bake at 400° 20 minutes or until chicken is no longer pink when slashed. Transfer to serving plate, Pass sauce, Serves 8.

SAUCE
Heat tomato sauce with chopped onion and cumin until hot. Season to taste with salt, pepper and liquid hot pepper seasoning.

CHICKEN TAMALE CASSEROLE
ALICE JONES

An old faithful. Many people have my recipe. Make and bake this casserole a day ahead.

2 cans of tamales, cut lengthwise
1/2 pound mushrooms, sliced
1 small can Mexican (or regular)
 tomato sauce
6 chicken breasts, cooked and boned
1½ cups cooked rice, with lime
 squeezed over it
2 bunches green onions, chopped,
 include tops
1/2 cup chopped cilantro
1 can olives, chopped
1 can green chilies, chopped
1 small can Mexican (or regular)
 tomato sauce
2 cans cream of chicken soup
Cheddar cheese, grated
cover with breadcrumbs and melted butter

Layer above in order listed in a baking pan. Bake 350° 45-60 minutes. Cool, refrigerate over night. Serve at room temperature with sour cream, avocado, salsa and tomatillo sauce.

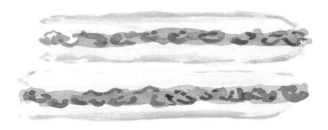

MEXICAN CHICKEN
MARY NOVAK

1 chicken, wrapped in foil and baked, re-serve juices
1 dozen corn tortillas, torn into pieces
1 can cream of mushroom soup
1 can cream of chicken soup
1 onion, finely chopped
1 cup milk
1 can red chili salsa
1 4-ounce can diced green chilies
1/2 pound Monterey Jack cheese, grated

Tear cooked chicken into pieces, remove bones. Combine soups, onion, milk, reserved juices, salsa and chilies. Layer chicken, sauce and cheese and repeat. Bake 350° 60 minutes. Serves 6-8

GREEN ENCHILADAS
BARBARA SHAFER

These Green Enchiladas were my children's (and now my grandchildren's) number one birthday dinner request. If you don't overcook, the spinach will hold its color and it makes a lovely presentation.

FILLING
4½ cups chicken breasts, cooked and pulled apart in bite-sized pieces
1 cup grated sharp Cheddar cheese
1 cup grated Monterey Jack cheese
SAUCE
2 cans cream of mushroom soup
1 4-ounce can Ortega diced chilies
1 large onion, diced
1 glove garlic, minced
1 can chicken broth
3/4 cup pureed raw spinach
1/2 teaspoon salt
2 tablespoons flour
12 corn tortillas

Puree mushroom soup, chilies, onion and garlic. Transfer to pan, add salt and chicken broth. Bring to boiling point and simmer for 10 minutes. Mix flour with a little water and pureed spinach – stir constantly, bring to boil again. Remove from heat. Soften tortillas in hot oil until soft and pliable. Drain on paper towels. Dip tortillas in sauce, coating on both sides. Place some chicken pieces and some of the cheeses along center of tortilla and roll up. Place seam side down in greased baking dish. Cover with remaining sauce and top with cheese. Bake 350° 20-30 minutes until well heated and cheese is melted. Serves 6. After plating, top enchiladas with minced green onions, guacamole (or slices of avocado), a dollop of sour cream and offer fresh or bottled red salsa.

Eating in St. Helena

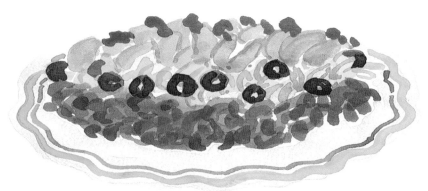

TAMALE CASSEROLE
MARY NOVAK

Mary did not give ingredient amounts. It's easy enough to figure out and can be doubled or tripled.

**white canned corn
tamales, canned, cut in 1/2" pieces
Cheddar cheese, cubes
canned tomatoes, drained
Monterey Jack cheese, cubed
Dennisons Chili
top with Frito Lay corn chips and olives**

Layer indredients. Bake 350• 40 minutes.

CHICKEN TORTILLA CASSEROLE
RUTHIE RYDMAN

**4 whole chicken breasts
8 corn tortillas
1 can cream of chicken soup
1 can cream mushroom soup
1 "soup can" milk
1 onion, grated
1 4-ounce can Ortega green chilies
1 pound Monterey Jack cheese, grated.**

Cook chicken breasts until tender and cut into serving pieces. Quarter tortillas. Put a small amount of chicken broth in bottom of 3 quart baking dish. Mix soups and water. Start with tortillas and layer ingredients topping with cheese. Refrigerate for 24 hours before baking. Bake 300° 60 minutes. Serves 6.

Eating in St. Helena

MEXICALI DELIGHT
ANNE CUTTING

Does it seem we work awfully hard to cook sophisticated food now, when our old favorites were pretty satisfying?

**Frito Lay corn chips
1 40-ounce can Dennison's chili, warmed
iceberg lettuce, chopped
tomatoes, onions, olives, avocado, chopped
Cheddar cheese, grated**

Place above ingredients in the order they appear above on individual plates and top with commercial Green Goddess dressing.

CILANTRO CHICKEN
MISSY DORAN

**4 chicken breasts, skinned and boned
1/4 cup lime juice
1/2 cup chopped cilantro
6 cloves garlic, chopped
1 tablespoon honey
1 tablespoon olive oil
1/2 teaspoon salt
1/2 teaspoon pepper
hot red pepper flakes, to taste**

Pound chicken breasts to an even thickness (about ½") and place in shallow baking pan. Mix lime juice, cilantro, garlic, honey, olive oil, salt, pepper and pepper flakes in a small bowl. Pour over chicken and turn pieces to coat evenly. Cover and chill at least 30 minutes or overnight. Lay chicken on grill over medium heat and cook turning only once, until no longer pink on inside about 4 to 6 minutes per side. Serves 4.

MEXICALI TAMALE PIE
CAROLYN PRIDE

This was my 1970's standby. I could always count on it being a success!

3 tablespoons vegetable oil
1½ cups chopped onions
1 clove garlic, mashed
1 green pepper, diced
1 pound ground round
1 12-ounce can whole kernel corn
1 small can sliced ripe olives, reserve some for top of casserole
1 tablespoon chili powder
1/2 teaspoon salt
several dashes Tabasco sauce
1/2 teaspoon ground pepper
2 8-ounce cans tomato sauce
1/2 pound Cheddar, grated
1½ cups yellow corn meal
1½ cups cold water
2½ cups boiling water
3/4 teaspoon salt
1 tablespoon butter

Sauté onions, garlic and green pepper in oil until soft. Remove from pan. Brown meat in remaining oil. Add next seven ingredients and cook 20 minutes. Stir corn meal into cold water. Add to boiling water. Add salt and butter and cook until thickened. Cover. Lower heat and cook 10 minutes more. Add 1 cup cheese to meat mixture and cook 5 minutes more. Spoon meat mixture into shallow casserole and spoon cornmeal in ring around the edge. Sprinkle with remaining cheese. Garnish with olives. Bake 375° 30 minutes.

SNAZZY MEXICAN DISH
SUSAN EDELEN

2 pounds lean ground round
1 large yellow onion, diced
2 28-ounce cans Las Palmas Red Chili sauce (no substitutions)
1 pound sharp Cheddar cheese, grated
1 package large flour tortillas
1 pint sour cream
1/2 can black olives, pitted

Sauté meat and onions and drain off fat. Cut tortillas into triangles. Layer meat mixture, tortillas, sour cream, sauce and cheese two times and top with olives.Bake 350° 45–60 minutes – until bubbly. Serves 6 to 8.

SPOONBREAD TAMALE PIE
SUSAN SMITH

Adapted from Sunset Cook Book of Favorite recipes 1969 edition.

1½ pounds ground chuck
1 large onion, chopped
1 green pepper, chopped
1 clove garlic, minced
1/4 cup olive oil
1 15–ounce can tomatoes or several fresh tomatoes, chopped
1 package frozen corn
2 teaspoons salt
4-6 teaspoons chili powder
1/4 teaspoon ground pepper
1/2 cup cornmeal
1 cup water
1 small can olives, chopped or sliced
cornmeal topping, recipe follows

Sauté meat, onion, green pepper and garlic together in heated oil until onions are golden, about 10 minutes. Stir in tomatoes, corn, salt, chili powder and pepper. Cover and simmer 5 minutes. Blend cornmeal with water and stir into the mixture. Simmer 10 minutes more. Add olives, and turn into a 9" X 13" baking dish. Cover with cornmeal topping.
CORNMEAL TOPPING
3 cups milk
1 teaspoon salt
1/4 cup butter
1 cup cornmeal
2 cups Cheddar cheese, grated
4 eggs, beaten

Scald milk with salt and butter. Gradually add cornmeal. Cook, stirring until thickened. Remove from heat, stir in cheese and beaten eggs. Bake uncovered 375° 40 minutes. Serves 8.

Eating in St. Helena

TAMALE CASSEROLE
MARYBETH EGNER

This is a tried and true favorite from the Wood/ Jack families. It was made by my grandmother, mother, aunts, sister and many times by me over the years. It was expected at holidays, picnics and special occasions. It fed a big crowd and was always considered an absolute favorite. I have three handwritten recipes for this, one in my mom's hand; one in my Aunt Helen's hand and one in my sister's hand. I think it was just handed down being remembered by heart mostly. The three recipes hardly differ.

1/3 cup oil or butter
1 large onion, chopped
1 28-ounce can tomatoes, chopped
1 cup corn meal
1 pound ground beef
2 eggs
1½ teaspoons salt
1/2 teaspoon pepper
1 teaspoon chili powder
1 15-ounce can creamed corn
1 can black olives, pitted and drained

Sauté onion in oil until golden. Add tomatoes. When hot stir in corn meal. Cook 10 minutes and remove from heat. Let cool. Add eggs, meat, corn, olives and seasonings. Blend well. Bake in greased heavy Dutch oven. I always used the old black, heavy as lead, well-seasoned Dutch oven that belonged to my mother. I never remember seeing this cooked in anything else. Bake 350° 45 - 60 minutes. This recipe was often doubled and fed up to 15 to 18 people (along with a ham or whatever else was being served.) In that case you want to let it cook 1½ - 2 hours at least. When you see it browning around the edges of the Dutch oven and getting crusty on top, it's ready to take out. Let it sit for a bit and then put it on the table right in the Dutch oven with a big serving spoon and watch it disappear. If there is any left, it is even better the next day.

ENCHILADAS
INGE HEINEMANN AND BARBARA SHURTZ

INGE'S RECIPE
This was originally from Joan Rombauer, circa 1974/75. We would spend a lot of time with our four children and their two children in the Heinemann Mountain Vineyard working and harvesting. Many meals were shared and this was one of our favorites.

1 28-ounce can mild enchilada sauce
1 can tomato sauce
1 green bell pepper, diced
dash of salt
1 pound ground beef, cooked or shredded cooked chicken
1 pound Cheddar cheese, grated
1 small can chopped olives
1 bunch green onions, chopped
1 dozen corn tortillas

Mix sauces and heat. Dip tortillas one at a time into sauce. Place on plate and fill with meat, olives, cheese, onions and roll up. Place in baking dish-seam down. Cover with sauce and more cheese. Bake 325° 30-35 minutes.

BARBARA'S RECIPE
2 pounds ground beef
2 tablespoons oil
1 large onion, chopped
1 can pitted olives
2 8-ounce cans tomato sauce
1 10-ounce can enchilada sauce
1 12-ounce can corn with pimento and pepper
1/4 pound Cheddar cheese, grated
1/2 teaspoon each rosemary, oregano and marjoram
1½ teaspoon chili powder dissolved in hot water
salt and pepper to taste
1 dozen corn tortillas

Sauté onion in oil. Reserve some for sauce. Add beef, cook until brown. Slice olives, keeping some whole for top. Add corn, sliced olives and seasonings. Combine sauces and pour half into meat mixture. Simmer 45 minutes. Soften tortillas by dipping in hot oil, then in sauce. Put 2 tablespoons meat and cheese on tortilla, roll up and place in casserole dish. Put olives, more sauce and cheese on top. Bake 350° 15-30 minutes until warm and cheese is melted.

MEXICAN ENCHILADAS
FAMILIA DE ANTONIO MANZO

corn tortillas
1 can Chili las Palmas Rojo
1 pound Cotija cheese
1 tablespoon sour cream per enchilada
1 pound potatoes
oil, coat pan
2 plus tablespoons butter
1 pound tomatoes
1/4 head Iceberg lettuce
1 pound cooked ham
1 or 2 chilies de Arbol
3 cloves garlic
salt to taste
pinch oregano

Boil potatoes. Cool and peel. Mash and add butter and salt. Grate cheese and put on plate with red chilies.

SALSA
Peel tomatoes and put in blender with garlic, oregano and salt, adding water if needed.

Wash and slice lettuce. Cut ham into 2" squares Heat one cup oil in heavy pan (cast iron preferred). First dip tortillas in Las Palmas red chili sauce. Place tortilla in hot oil and add potatoes, fold over tortilla and switch to a hot griddle turning frequently cooking until they get crisp. Place enchiladas onto plate, cover with cheese, lettuce and a couple of slices of ham. Add sour cream at center and then the salsa.

THREE BEAN CASSEROLE
VALERIE PRESTEN

I can't tell you how many times I have made this, especially to take to a potluck. It's easy, can be made ahead, doubled, frozen – it's foolproof. I have never brought home my casserole with even one bean left. This is the recipe I use, somewhat altered from the original. Amounts are approximate, use more or less of any ingredient, depending upon your taste.

1 package frozen lima or edamame beans
3 1 pound-3 ounce cans baked beans, about 6 cups
3 15½-ounce cans kidney beans, about 5 cups
1 pound Italian link sausages or pork sausages
1/2 cup ham, 1/2" cubes
1 large onion, chopped
SAUCE (adjust to your taste)
1 8-ounce can tomato sauce
1/2 cup catsup
1/4 cup brown sugar
1 tablespoon salt
1 teaspoon pepper
1 teaspoon dry mustard

Heat oven to 400°. Cut up sausages and brown. Mix with remaining ingredients and gently stir in sauce. Bake uncovered 400° 60 minutes. Serves 10 to 12.

JOHNNY M CASSEROLE
DIANE LIVINGSTON

A kid's favorite.

1 medium onion
1 pound ground beef
1 package Sloppy Joe mix
1 small can corn niblets
1 16-ounce can tomato sauce
1 cup macaroni
1 cup grated Cheddar cheese

Sauté onion until translucent, add ground beef and brown. Mix in Sloppy Joe mix, tomato sauce and drained corn niblets. Cook macaroni, drain and add to mixture. Put in casserole and top with Cheddar. May be baked immediately or frozen for future use. Bake 300° 45 minutes.

Eating in St. Helena

FIRESIDE CASSEROLE
SALLY TANTAU

2 pounds ground beef
1 8-ounce package noodles, cooked
1 cup sour cream
1 cup cottage cheese
1 large package Philadelphia cream cheese
2 heaping tablespoons chopped green pepper
2 heaping tablespoons chopped green onions
2 8-ounce cans Hunt's tomato sauce
3 tablespoons melted butter

Lightly brown meat, season and add cooked noodles and one can tomato sauce to meat. Mix cheeses, sour cream, chopped onions and peppers. Butter 2 quart casserole. Place half meat, noodle mixture on bottom, cheese mixture next and rest of meat, noodles. Top with melted butter. Let stand several hours or over night. Bake 375° 50 minutes. During last 10 minutes of baking time add second can of tomato sauce on top. Serves 8.

JUICY BURGERS
SIENA O'CONNELL

My mom did this when we were kids. They are so good!

Iceberg lettuce, shredded
ketchup
mayonnaise
ground beef

Mix mayonaise and ketchup. Combine with shredded lettuce. Pile on cooked hamburgers.

FLAMING HAM
MARIANNE PETERSEN

A festive presentation for Christmas Eve and other occasions. Proportions are for a 7 pound ham.

1 cup brown sugar
2 tablespoons flour
1/2 teaspoon cloves, crushed
2 tablespoons water

Spread above on ham 30 minutes before ham is finished cooking. After ham is just out of the oven spread on
1/3 cup brown sugar moistened with
2 tablespoons orange extract

Ignite warm brandy and spoon over ham. Serves 12- 14.

LUCY'S NEVER FAIL
BEEF TENDERLOIN
LUCY SHAW

A Christmas treat.

1 beef tenderloin – carefully weighed and at room temperature
sesame oil
fresh ground pepper, medium grind

Preheat oven to 500°. Pat meat dry. Rub with sesame oil. Dredge heavily all over with ground black pepper. Place on rack over baking pan. Put in 500° oven for **exactly 3 minutes per pound.** Turn oven off. **DO NOT OPEN DOOR.** Meat will be perfect in 1 hour and 45 minutes.

HAMBURGER STROGANOFF
NANCY MORRELL

A walk down memory lane and simpler times.

1/2 cup minced onion
1/4 cup butter
1 clove garlic, minced
1 pound ground beef
2 tablespoons flour
2 teaspoons salt
1/4 teaspoon pepper
1 pound fresh mushrooms, sliced or
1 8-ounce can, sliced mushrooms
1 can cream of chicken soup
1 cup sour cream
2 tablespoons minced parsley
6 ounces dry noodles, cooked al dente

Sauté onion and garlic in butter over medium heat. Add meat and brown. Add flour, salt, pepper and mushrooms. Cook 5 minutes. Add soup, simmer uncovered 10 minutes. Stir in sour cream. Heat through. Serve over noodles. Serves 4 to 6.

MUSHROOM BURGERS
BECKY PARRIOTT

This one one of my mother's recipes.

3 eggs
1 onion, shredded
1/2 teaspoon poultry seasoning
1 envelope vegetable broth seasoning
1 4-ounce can chopped mushrooms
 -drain and save liquid
2 cups Quaker Oats, uncooked
2 tablespoons margarine, melted
1 can mushroom soup

Mix all ingredients together and make into patties and fry in melted margarine. Place in a greased casserole. Mix mushroom soup, liquid from mushrooms with enough water to 1/2 cup and 1 envelope vegetable broth seasoning. Pour over patties. Bake 350° 30 to 60 minutes.

LADDIE'S MEAT LOAF
LADDIE HALL

Laddie says it's the molasses that brings everyone back for seconds with this meat loaf.

1 cup sliced mushrooms
1/2 onion, chopped
1 egg, slightly beaten
1/2 cup milk
1½ teaspoons Worcestershire sauce
1 teaspoon salt
1/2 teaspoon dry mustard
several "grinds" pepper
1½ cups soft bread crumbs
1½ pounds LMR grass-fed ground beef
4 tablespoons catsup
2 tablespoons molasses
2-3 eggs, hard boiled (optional)

Preheat oven to 350°. In a mixing bowl combine milk, lightly beaten egg, Worcestershire sauce, seasonings and bread crumbs. Let stand about 5 minutes. Stir in ground beef, chopped mushrooms and onions. Mix lightly, but thoroughly. Peel hard boiled eggs. Shape meat mixture into loaf placing eggs in center. Place in a 9" x 13" x 2" pan. Bake 60 minutes. Remove from oven. Combine molasses and catsup, brush on meat loaf and return to bake 10 more minutes. Makes a tasty glaze.
To serve, slice to reveal egg in center. Garnish with parsley.

CAJUN MEATLOAF
BETSY HOLZHAUER

2 onions, chopped
2 cloves garlic, minced
2 tablespoons oil
1/2 cup cornbread crumbs, or plain breadcrumbs
2 pounds ground beef
1 egg, slightly beaten
1/4 cup chopped parsley
1 8-ounce can tomato sauce
3/4 teaspoon each cumin and
red pepper flakes
1/2 teaspoon each thyme and sage
1 green bell pepper, diced
4 ounces each Cheddar and Mozzarella cheese, grated
salt

Sauté onions and garlic. Mix remaining ingredients except cheese with onions and garlic. Put half of meat mixture in oiled loaf pan. Top with half combined cheeses. Fill pan with remaining meat mixture. Lay remaining cheese on top. Bake 350° 90 minutes. Pour off liquid. Serves 8.

Eating in St. Helena

WHITE RIVER REUBEN ROLL
CAROLYN PRIDE

This excellent - even company worthy meatloaf comes from the 1987 Créme de Colorado cookbook. I've made it many times.

1½ pound ground beef (use good quality)
1½ cups fresh caraway rye bread crumbs (about 3 slices pulsed in blender)
1/2 cup (heaping) finely chopped onion
1 egg, lightly beaten
1/4 cup Thousand Island Dressing (made as follows - combine)
> **2 tablespoons mayonaise**
> **2 tablespoons catsup**
> **1 tablespoon sweet pickle relish**

1 tablespoon Worcestershire Sauce
1½ teaspoons salt
1/4 teaspoon pepper, freshly ground
1 14-ounce can sauerkraut, well drained
1½ cups grated Swiss cheese

In large bowl combine beef, bread crumbs, egg, onion, Thousand Island Dressing, Worcestershire, salt and pepper. Work with hands until well blended. Shape into 6" x 14" rectangle on a sheet of waxed paper. Sprinkle with sauerkraut and Swiss cheese, leaving a 1" border on all sides. Start with narrow end and roll into loaf letting waxed paper be guide. Place in shallow pan. Bake, uncovered 350° 45 minutes. Let rest a few minutes before slicing. Serves 6.

DRAGON DOGS
DIANA STOCKTON

My children are all excellent cooks. My eldest is especially good. He began cooking early in his life and is now a real artist. He was 8 years old when he got the idea for Dragon Dogs. Of course, he says, we carved our names all the time in hot dogs before cooking. That was standard. He got to thinking of how the cuts looked as they cooked - how they opened up. He was an admirer of dinosaurs and dragons, so the "aha" moment came one day at lunch.

at least 1 hot dog per person
butter
soy sauce (optional)
frozen peas

Make quick, shallow cuts in each hot dog, turning as you cut, as though it were a smooth fish you were giving scales to. Not too deep or you will sunder it. Cook in melted butter, with a few dashes of soy sauce moving it about until nicely dark all over and the scales have opened, revealing a pale interior. Serve with a helping of what our household calls "orange noodles," but you may know as Kraft Macroni and Cheese or Annie's Naturals or some such. Frozen peas are another good choice. Eating frozen clumps while waiting for the dragons to cook is very pleasant and cooked peas look most attractive on the plate. You can also lay the dragon on a roll and provide the usual accompaniments. But, a Dragon Dog is especially good on its own.

NOTE: On optional soy sauce. The original version included quite a bit more than a dash of soy sauce, producing a dramatic loud of black smoke, quite a thick, salty taste glaze at the tip of each fish scale and a nearly impossible to clean pan at the finish. If you are a real purist, and find these additional qualities desirable, then by all means, use more soy.

BEEF FONDUE WITH SAUCES
JUDIE ROGERS

A popular dinner party treat.

2 cups cooking oil
1 ½ to 2 pounds tender beef, cut into 3/4"
cubes

Bring oil to table heated and continue heating on top of fondue burner. Spear meat with fondue forks and dip into hot oil. Oil must be hot enough to sizzle. Meat will only take a few minutes to cook. Use a second fork to eat. Serve with sauces.

HONG KONG SAUCE

1/3 cup soy sauce
1 teaspoon ground ginger
3 tablespoons oil
1 teaspoon dry mustard
1 tablespoon sugar
4 cloves garlic, minced
dash salt, pepper, cayenne pepper

Stir mustard into soy sauce until smooth. Combine with remaining ingredients in a small saucepan. Heat to boiling and serve hot.

MUSTARD SAUCE

1/2 cup mayonaise
1/4 cup Dijon mustard

Combine and mix well.

CURRIED MAYONIASE

1/3 cup lemon juice
1/4 teaspoon dry mustard
1/2 teaspoon salt
1 egg
1 cup olive oil
1 tablespoon curry powder

Place lemon juice, mustard, salt, egg, 1/4 cup oil and curry powder in blender. Turn to low speed and gradually put in remaining oil in a steady stream. Place in bowl and serve.

CAPER BUTTER

1/2 cup softened butter
3 tablespoons capers with liquid

Combine and beat until light and fluffy. Place in bowl and serve.

Eating in St. Helena

PORCUPINE MEATBALLS
SHERLYN ZUMWALT

Our daughter, Lori, often mentions this recipe. She liked the name more than anything.

1 egg, beaten.
1 10¾-ounce can condensed tomato soup
1/4 cup long grain rice
2 tablespoons chopped onion
1 tablespoon chopped parsley
1/2 teaspoon salt
1/8 teaspoon pepper
1 pound ground beef
1 teaspoon Worcestershire sauce

Combine egg and 1/4 cup of soup. Stir in un-cooked rice, onion, parsley, salt and pepper. Add meat and mix well, shape into 20 small balls. Place in 10" skillet. Mix remaining soup, Worcestershire sauce and 1/2 cup water. Add to skillet. Bring to boiling, reduce heat, cover and simmer 35-40 minutes. Stir often. Serves 4 or 5.

GO TO THE AIRPORT STEW
ANNE CUTTING

We called this Go to the Airport Stew because I could put it in the oven and we'd drive to the airport to pick up Cecil's mom and come home to dinner, ready to eat. I think it was originally called Stay in Bed Stew.

1½ pounds stew meat
4 carrots, cut up
4 stalks celery, cut-up
3 potatoes, quartered
1 green pepper, cut up
2 cans cream of mushroom soup
1 package onion soup mix
ground pepper

Place in above order in covered casserole. Bake 250° 5 hours.

VINTNERS' STEW
KATHLEEN PATTERSON

One of my favorite recipes that I use over and over is Vintners' Stew. I got it from one of the first wine cookbooks, Favorite Recipes of California Winemakers. Paul Huber of E. & J Gallo contributed this to the book. It is a good old standby that gets rave reviews even in today's gourmet environment. I may have deviated from the original recipe, but this is what I do today. It's especially great because it all goes in one pot, cooks slowly with wonderful aromas emanating from the kitchen.

1½ to 2 pounds beef stew meat
2 cans beef consommé
1/2 bottle red wine
1 large or 2 medium yellow onions, sliced
1/2 cup flour
1/2 cup bread crumbs
salt
pepper
garlic salt to taste

Combine beef, wine, consommé, salts, pepper and onion in a heavy casserole. Mix flour with crumbs, stir into meat mixture. Cover. Bake 325° several hours (4 to 5) until meat is tender. Just before serving stir in 1/4 cup wine for additional wine flavor.

Eating in St. Helena

61

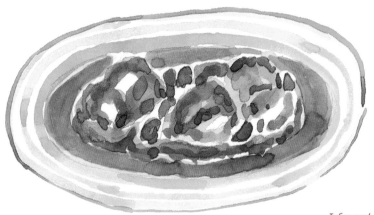

OLD FASHIONED BEEF STEW
TONI NICHELINI IRWIN

1/4 cup all-purpose flour
1 teaspoon salt
1 teaspoon paprika
1/2 teaspoon coarse ground pepper
2 pounds boneless chuck, cut into
 1" cubes
1/2 pound Crimini mushrooms, sliced
1 tablespoon olive oil
3 cups beef broth, homemade or canned
1 cup good red wine
2 bay leaves
1 teaspoon thyme
1 onion, chopped coarsely
4 carrots, cut in 1/4" rounds
6 medium red potatoes, peeled and cut into
1" cubes
2 tablespoons chopped parsley

Combine flour, salt, paprika, pepper in bowl.
Dredge meat in mixture. Heat 5 quart Dutch oven
over med-high heat; add oil, meat and brown
well. Add wine, deglaze and burn off alcohol. Add
mushrooms, mix well. Cook about 1½ minutes.
Add broth, bay leaves and thyme. Bring to boil,
cover and simmer about 1¼ hours. Add onion
and carrots, simmer 10 minutes. Add potatoes,
cover and simmer 20 to 25 minutes. Discard bay
leaves. Ladle into bowls and sprinkle with parsley.
Serving suggestion: Hollow out small round
loaves of French bread to use as bowls.

BEEF SHORT RIBS
AND KIDNEY BEANS
SANDRA PICKETT

*I found this recipe in a magazine in 1964-65 and
have been making it regularly ever since. When
each Pickett left for college and later, the real
world, I gathered lists of 3 favorite meals and
3 desserts. Beef Ribs and Kidney Beans was the
only one common to all three kid's lists. I am list-
ing the original recipe first and then my changes
later.*

4 pounds short ribs, each 2½" - 3"
1 large onion, sliced
1 clove garlic, chopped
2 tablespoons shortening
1 tablespoon salt
fresh ground pepper
1 teaspoon thyme
2 tablespoons chili powder
1 cup red wine or beef stock
2 16-ounce cans red kidney beans, rinsed
and drained

Preheat oven to 450°. Melt shortening in large
casserole or baking pan with lid. Put onion and
garlic across bottom, then beef ribs, bone side
down. Season with salt, pepper and thyme. Bake
uncovered 30 minutes. Turn ribs and bake 20
minutes longer. Reduce oven to 350°. Drain off
all fat and discard. Sprinkle ribs with chili powder,
add wine or stock. Cover tightly and bake 60 minutes. Add beans and bake 30 minutes more or until beans are hot. Serves 6. The recipe suggested
serving this over rice, accompanied by a tart cole
slaw and crusty country bread. I've always done
that! A perfect combo!

MY CHANGES
I use 4 to 5 cloves garlic and 4 tablespoons chili
powder. I add garlic with the chili powder. 450°
is too hot for garlic. I add 1 or 2 more onions, more
thyme and more wine.Sometimes I make my own
kidney beans. Use 3 cans of beans if serving 6
adult hearty eaters. This is a great meal for family
and guests. I just turn oven to 275° and leave it
4 to 5 hours. No matter which temperature used,
the pot must be tightly sealed.

Eating in St. Helena

RISOTTO
EVALYN TRINCHERO

1/4 cup butter
2 ounces salt pork, diced
2 tablespoons oil
3/4 pound onion, peeled and diced
4 chicken livers, fresh or frozen, finely chopped
3 cups chicken broth, boiling – more if needed
1/8 teaspoon ground saffron
1/2 teaspoon salt
1/3 teaspoon ground black pepper
1 cup uncooked rice
Parmesan cheese, grated

Place butter, salt pork and olive oil in skillet and heat. Add onions and cook until medium brown. Add chopped livers, salt, and pepper. Stir and brown for 5 minutes. Add rice, stir well and cook for 2 minutes. Add boiling broth. Stir well, cover and simmer 18 minutes. Test for doneness and add more salt if needed. Add saffron and stir. If rice is too dry add more broth. Serve on warm plates. Sprinkle with grated Parmesan cheese. Serves 4 to 6.

JANICE'S RISOTTO
JANICE MONDAVI AND SIENA O'CONNELL

An easy microwave recipe.

2 tablespoons olive or Porcini oil
2 tablespoons butter
1 chopped onion
Microwave 4 minutes
ADD
1 cup Arborio rice
Microwave 4 minutes
ADD
3 cups chicken broth
Microwave 9 minutes
Stir
Microwave 9 minutes more
ADD
salt
pepper
Parmesan cheese

OPTIONAL
Add sautéed mushrooms or other vegetables

PORK-PERSIMMON RISOTTO
HAROLYN THOMPSON

My garden has a prolific Fuju persimmon tree, so when Sunset Magazine was looking for recipes that used persimmons, I developed this one. I usually pass a dish with extra persimmon pieces and blue cheese. Earlier in the summer, peaches substitute beautifully for the persimmons.

2 cups chicken broth, low salt
1¼ cups white wine, Riesling, Chenin Blanc or unoaked Chardonnay
3 tablespoons butter
3 tablespoons olive oil
2 shallots, about 3 tablespoons, finely minced
1/2 pound boneless pork cut into ½" cubes (chops, steak or tenderloin all work)
1 cup Arborio rice or medium grain Pearl rice
1/2 teaspoon allspice
1/4 teaspoon freshly ground black pepper
1 large or 2 medium Fuyu persimmons, (firm/ripe) cut into bite size wedges
1 ounce blue cheese, coarsely grated
2 tablespoons chopped Italian parsley

Heat broth and wine in saucepan over medium-low heat. Heat butter and olive oil in a 3 quart sauté pan or Dutch oven and add shallots and sauté until soft, 8 to 10 minutes. Remove shallots to small dish with slotted spoon. Raise heat to medium and add pork cubes and cook until no longer pink. Add to shallot dish. Add rice to sauté pan, cook and stir 3 to 4 minutes until it turns golden. Mix in allspice and pepper. Stir in 1 cup hot wine/broth, cook and stir over medium–high heat until broth is absorbed. Add remaining broth one cup at a time and cook as above. When all liquid has been added and rice is tender and creamy, stir in shallots and pork. Cover, turn heat to low, cook 2 minutes. Uncover, stir, and add persimmons. Heat 2 more minutes.
Serve on heated plates or bowls. Garnish with chopped parsley around outer edge and grated blue cheese in center. Serves 2-3 main course or 4-6 accompaniment servings.

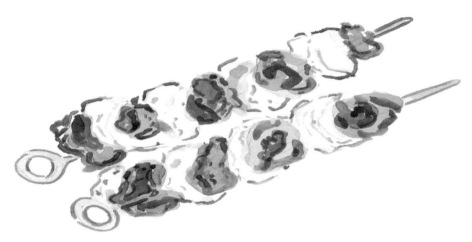

GRILLED, BUTTERFLIED
LEG OF LAMB
SUE FOGARTY

leg of lamb, butterflied
2 ounces Scotch whiskey
3 ounces sherry
1 cup orange juice
1 teaspoon A1 sauce
1 teaspoon Worcestershire sauce
garlic salt to taste
salt and pepper to taste

Combine ingredients in pan large enough to lay lamb flat. Marinate 6 to 8 hours turning every 2 hours. Remove lamb from marinade. Barbeque on hot grill 20 minutes per side, basting with reserved marinade.

LAMB SHANKS
BEV POPKO

4 lamb shanks
2 cloves garlic
salt and freshly ground pepper
1/2 teaspoon each basil, oregano, rosemary and thyme
1/2 teaspoon curry powder
1 bay leaf, crumbled
4 large onions, thinly sliced
2 tablespoons soy sauce
1/2 cup red wine

Preheat oven to 400°. Rub lamb shanks with garlic. Place in roasting pan and sprinkle with salt and pepper. Mix together herbs, curry powder and baby leaf and sprinkle over meat. Place sliced onions on top of lamb and pour soy sauce over the top. Roast, uncovered, for 15 minutes, reduce heat to 300° and roast 2 more hours. Pour off fat, then add wine. Cover and roast 1 hour more. Serve with rice or scalloped potatoes. Serves 4.

SHISH KEBAB AND PILAF
PATTY VASCONI

I grew up in the Central Valley with many Armenian neighbors and this was always served. We made this many times for our square dance group in St. Helena. Ernie Navone let us put the marinating lamb in his meat locker.

leg of lamb, cut in 1" chunks
1 teaspoon oregano
1 large clove garlic, minced
2 medium onions, sliced
at least a wineglass full of sherry wine
1/2 to 3/4 cup olive oil

Put all ingredients together, mix well. Marinate overnight in refrigerator. Place meat on skewers and barbeque or broil turning to brown on all sides.

PILAF
1/4 pound butter
1/2 cup figure eight Vermicelli
1 cup rice
2 cups boiling water
salt

Brown vermicelli in butter . Add washed and drained rice and brown. Add boiling water and salt. Cover, lower heat, simmer until done.

ALMOND AND RAISIN TOPPING
1/2 cup almonds
1/2 cup raisins
2 tablespoons butter

Blanch almonds. Put a small amount of butter in heavy skillet, add raisins, almonds and a little water. Add about 1 teaspoon sugar. Cover and steam until raisins are soft. Pour over pilaf.

Eating in St. Helena

SPICY POLENTA LASANGA
SYLVIA PESTONI

8 ounces sweet Italian sausages
1 medium onion, diced
1 14½-ounce can tomatoes, diced
1 teaspoon Tabasco sauce
2 tablespoons butter
1 8-ounce tube prepared polenta, cut into
1/2' slices
1 cup grated Mozzarella or Fontina cheese
1/4 cup grated Parmesan cheese

Preheat oven to 400°. Remove casing from sausages, break up meat and cook until well browned in a 12" skillet over medium-high heat, stirring occasionally. Remove sausage to bowl. Cook onions in remaining drippings until softened. Add to bowl with sausage. Stir in tomatoes and their liquid and hot pepper sauce. Melt one tablespoon butter in same skillet. Cook polenta slices, half at a time, until browned on both sides. Repeat with remaining butter and polenta slices. Spoon half of the sausage mixture into a 9" x 9" baking dish. Top with half of the polenta slices and half of the Mozzarella and Parmesan cheeses. Repeat layer again ending with cheeses. Bake 400° 20 minutes until cheese is melted and mixture is hot and bubbly. Serves 4.

LASAGNA
GERI RAYMOND

We have served and enjoyed this lasagna for over 40 years. Walter saw this recipe in The Napa Register in a section titled "For Men Only" not long after we were married in 1964. We have been serving it to family and friends ever since.

1 pound ground beef
2 cloves garlic, minced
1 6-ounce can tomato paste
2 1-pound 4-ounce cans tomatoes
1 package Lawry's Spaghetti Sauce mix
1/2 pound lasagna noodles, cooked
1/2 pound Mozzarella cheese, sliced
3/4 pound Ricotta cheese
1/2 cup grated Parmesan cheese

Brown ground beef and garlic in 2 tablespoons olive oil. Season with salt and pepper and simmer slowly about 10 minutes. Add tomato paste, tomatoes and spaghetti sauce mix. Stir throughly, cover and simmer 30 minutes. Boil noodles, drain and rinse well. Arrange a layer of meat sauce in bottom of oblong casserole. Cover with a layer of lasagna noodles then a layer of Mozzarella and dot with Ricotta cheese. Repeat layers ending with a layer of noodles covered with meat sauce. Sprinkle top generously with Parmesan cheese. Bake 375° 20 minutes.

Eating in St. Helena

POLENTA WITH BEEF AND SAUSAGE STEW
EVALYN TRINCHERO

These recipes were part of a cookbook we put together for St. Helena Parochial School more than 30 years ago. Can you believe I used salt pork or chicken livers? This was before we started trying to eat for our health. The family enjoyed these recipes very much, but I haven't prepared them in 20 years.

1½ pounds lean beef
3/4 pound sweet Italian sausage
2 garlic cloves, mashed
10 parsley sprigs, leaves only
1/2 pound fresh mushrooms or
1/2 ounce dried mushrooms
3 tablespoons olive oil
1/4 cup butter
2 ounces salt pork, diced
1/2 pound onions, peeled and diced
1/4 teaspoon freshly ground pepper
1 bay leaf, crumbled
1/2 cup white wine
2 tablespoons minced celery
2 tablespoons minced carrots
1 medium fresh tomato or 1/2 cup canned peeled plum tomatoes, finely chopped
1/2 cup hot water
pinch freshly grated nutmeg
salt to taste

Cut beef into 1/2" cubes, remove casing from sausage and cut meat into 1" pieces. Chop garlic and parsley together until almost pureed. Thinly slice mushrooms or use 1/2 ounce dried mushrooms soaked in lukewarm water 15 minutes. Drain, saving water, and chop. Combine oil, butter and salt pork in saucepan and heat. Add onions and sauté slowly until medium brown. Add beef and sausage and brown for 10 minutes. Add garlic, parsley, pepper and bay leaf. Stir and cook 10 minutes. Add wine, stir, cover and simmer 10 minutes. Add celery, carrot, tomatoes and mushrooms. Stir and cook 10 more minutes. Add water from dried mushrooms (if used). Stir, cover and cook 40 minutes. Grate nutmeg over the top and simmer 10 minutes more. Test beef for doneness. Add salt if needed. Serve over hot polenta. This is good with Sutter Home's Zinfandel. Serves 4-6.

ORIGINAL JOE'S SPECIAL
JOAN WESTGATE AND BARBARA SHURTZ

JOAN'S JOE'S SPECIAL
2 tablespoons olive or vegetable oil
2 pounds lean ground beef
2 medium onions, finely chopped
2 garlic cloves, finely minced
1/2 pound mushrooms, sliced
1¼ teaspoons salt
1/4 teaspoon ground nutmeg
1/4 teaspoon dry oregano
1/4 teaspoon pepper
1 10-ounce package frozen chopped spinach, thawed and squeezed dry; or 1/2 pound fresh spinach, rinsed, stems removed, and leaves chopped (about 4 cups)
4 to 6 large eggs, lightly beaten

Heat oil in a wide frying pan over high heat. Crumble in beef and cook, stirring often, until browned. Drain excess fat. Add onions, garlic and mushrooms; reduce heat to medium and cook, stirring occasionally, until onions are softened, about 5 minutes. Stir in salt, nutmeg, pepper, oregano and spinach; cook for about 5 more minutes. Add eggs. Reduce heat to low and cook, stirring constantly, just until eggs are softly set. Serves 6.

BARBARA'S JOE'S SPECIAL
I made Original Joe's Special many, many times while our kids were growing up. The recipe changed somewhat through the years. The "Special" started with instant onions and garlic, frozen spinach, canned mushrooms and frozen hash browns but evolved into fresh vegetables and leaner beef or chicken. Rich has noticed that I like to chop a lot !!!

1 onion, diced
1 pound ground beef
spinach
garlic, diced
mushrooms, sliced
leftover potatoes, cooked, optional
5 or 6 eggs
salt and pepper to taste

Sauté onion in oil. Add diced garlic. Brown ground beef and mix with onions and garlic. Season with salt and pepper. Steam and chop fresh spinach or use one package chopped frozen spinach, heated and drained completely. Lightly beat eggs. Add drained spinach and eggs to meat mixture and stir until scrambled. (The scrambling might take longer than you think.) Add mushrooms and/or potatoes to mix or sauté separately in a little butter or oil. Serves 3 or 4.

BROCCOLI AND ITALIAN SAUSAGE PASTA
HELEN DAKE

Everyone in our family liked this. The Italian sausage from Ernie's Meat Market in Kellers made it special. I still can remember how that sausage smelled as it cooked. This recipe originally came from Eating Well in a Busy World by Francine Allen (one of my favorite cookbooks when our sons were little) but I have simplified it some.

1 bunch broccoli
1 tablespoon olive oil
1 pound sweet Italian sausage (good Italian sausage, not prepackaged)
1 medium yellow onion, chopped
4 large cloves garlic, minced or pressed
2 bell peppers, (red if possible) cut into 1/4" strips
3 tablespoons pine nuts
1 tablespoon vermouth (or white wine)
12 ounces any pasta shapes
Parmesan cheese, grated

Prepare broccoli by cutting off and dividing flowerlets. Peel tough outer skin from stem and cut into bite-sized pieces. In a pot large enough to boil water for the pasta, steam broccoli until tender crisp. Rinse under cold water and drain. Cook pasta. Remove sausage from casings. Sauté sausage in 1 tablespoon olive oil, while breaking it into small bits. When it is golden, stir in onion, garlic and pepper. When onion is soft, stir in broccoli, pine nuts and vermouth. Cover and reduce heat. Sauté only until broccoli is heated through. When pasta is cooked al dente, drain and rinse under hot water. When thoroughly drained, add to vegetables and sausage and toss. If it seems dry add a little olive oil. Serve immediately and pass lots of Parmesan cheese.

TUNA NOODLE BAKE
SHERLYN ZUMWALT

Scott loved this dish, however his new family does not. Karen will make it for him sometimes and also, I do. It's still his dad Dave's favorite dish.

6 ounces extra wide noodles,
 uncooked yields 4½ cups cooked noodles
1 can cream of mushroom soup
1¼ cups milk
1/3 cup grated Parmesan or Romano cheese
1 9½-ounce can tuna, drained and flaked
salt and ground pepper to taste
corn chips, crumbled

Preheat oven to 350°. Cook noodles according to package directions for 4 minutes. Drain. In buttered 2 quart casserole dish combine soup, milk, cheese, tuna, salt and pepper. Stir in hot noodles. Add crumbled corn chips on top. and bake uncovered. Bake 25-30 minutes until bubbly and lightly browned. Serves 4

MACARONI AND CHEESE
CONNIE KAY

1 tablespoons butter
1 tablespoon flour
1 cup milk
1½ cups grated sharp Cheddar cheese
(white Canadian preferred)
8 ounces macaroni, cooked
Parmesan cheese, grated
breadcrumbs
salt and pepper

Butter casserole. Make a butter and flour roux, do not brown. Add milk and when hot add half the grated Cheddar cheese. Layer macaroni and remaining Cheddar (usually 2 layers). Add half of sauce after each layer. Top with bread crumbs and Parmesan. Dot with butter. Bake 350° 30-40 minutes until brown on top.

MACARONI AND CHEESE
SIENA O'CONNELL

macaroni
sharp Cheddar cheese, cubed
sour cream
milk
ham, cubed (may be added)

Cook desired amount of macaroni. Layer macaroni, cheese, salt and pepper, sour cream, milk and repeat. Finish with sour cream. Sprinkle with paprika. Bake 350° 60 minutes or until a good bubble is going.

BAKED ZITI
LYNETTE BENSEN

This recipe is asked for often it is easy and good as a side dish or a main course. It freezes and travels well. As each of my children had a new baby I made about a dozen dinners that freeze well ahead so when they came home from the hospital they would have dinner ready for a few days. This is one of their favorites.

1/2 pound Ziti macaroni, cooked
SAUCE
1/4 cup butter
1/4 cup flour
1 teaspoon salt
1/2 teaspoon pepper
2 cups milk
1/4 cup grated Parmesan cheese

Melt butter in medium sauce pan, remove from heat stir in flour, salt and pepper.
Add milk. Bring to a boil stirring, reduce heat simmer 1 minute. Remove from heat
add 1/4 cup Parmesan cheese, combine with cooked Ziti.
CHEESE LAYER:
1 pint creamed cottage cheese
1/4 cup grated Parmesan cheese
1 egg
1 tablespoon chopped parsley
1/2 teaspoon salt
1/2 teaspoon pepper

TOP
1/4 pound Mozzarella cheese. grated

Combine cheese layer ingredients in food processor. In 9" x 13" pan layer half Ziti mixture, all of the cheese mixture and then other half Ziti mixture. Sprinkle with grated Mozzarella cheese and paprika. Bake 350 ° uncovered 30 – 35 minutes.
NOTE: Can be topped with ½ to 1 pound cooked bulk sausage - added before the Mozzarella cheese.

FRESH PASTA WITH PROSCIUTTO, MUSHROOMS AND CREAM
KATHY CHELINI

This is a recipe we have been enjoying at our home with family and friends for many years. The most fun is making a mess rolling out the fresh pasta. Each of our children would take a turn at cranking the machine to roll out the dough. To their great surprise, after boiling their creation turned into tender delicious pasta. Now our grandchildren have taken over the job of rolling the pasta dough.

BASIC PASTA RECIPE (about one pound)
2 cups flour
3 eggs

Mound flour onto a large wooden board. Make a well in center of the flour and add eggs. Using a fork, beat the eggs and incorporate into flour. Once mixed, begin to knead dough into a ball. You may add a little more flour or pinch of water to make dough more workable. Knead dough for a least 10 minutes. Wrap in plastic and let rest 30 minutes. Break dough into 4-6 pieces. Cover. Flatten one piece on a floured board then roll out as thin as possible or use a pasta machine. Cut Fettuccine into 1/4" to 1/2" strips.

CREAM SAUCE
2 or more tablespoons olive oil or butter
4 ounces prosciutto or Italian Pancetta, chopped
2 cloves, garlic, chopped
1/2 pound fresh mushrooms, sliced
1 cup rich chicken stock
2 ounces dried Porcini mushrooms, re-hydrated in stock or water
1 cup Italian Dry Vermouth or dry white wine
1/2 to 3/4 pint heavy cream
3 tablespoons chopped fresh basil
pinch fresh nutmeg, ground
salt and pepper to taste
Parmesan Cheese for grating

Heat a large sauté pan. Add prosciutto, butter and/or olive oil. Sauté lightly, add garlic and cook until golden. Turn up heat, add fresh mushrooms, cook until they have given off most of their water. (If mushrooms do not seem to have a lot of moisture, you may need to add more butter or olive oil. Add wine, bring to boil and reduce by half. Reduce heat, add chicken stock and re-hydrated mushrooms along with their soaking liquid. Simmer for a few minutes, reduce heat to low, add cream, basil, nutmeg, salt and pepper to taste. Simmer to warm, do not let boil. Bring 6 quarts water and 2 tablespoons salt to a boil in a large pot. Drop fresh pasta into boiling water, cook until al dente. Minutes only. Drain pasta and place onto a pre-warmed platter. Top with the warm sauce. Serve with freshly grated Parmesan cheese.
OPTIONAL: For an additional bite, sprinkle a pinch of hot red pepper flakes or squeeze a couple of cloves of fresh garlic through a press into the sauce just before topping pasta.

Eating in St. Helena

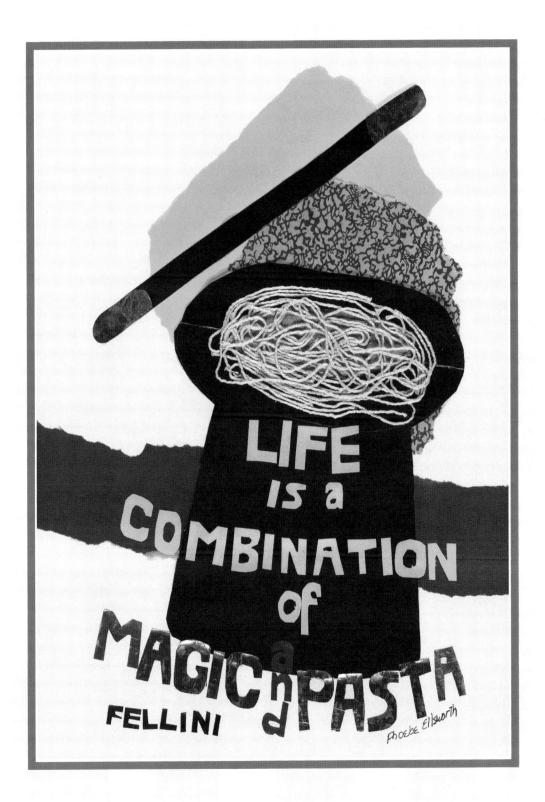

Sauces and Condiments

IT'S A COMFORTING SORT OF THING TO HAVE

JAM

CHUTNEY

sauce

relish

Christopher Robin
Winnie the Pooh
A. A. Milne

BLACKBERRY CATSUP
HAROLYN THOMPSON

The abundance of wild blackberries around St. Helena caused me to create this recipe. It is sweet-tart and spicy. It clings well when spooned onto pork, lamb, poultry or burgers. It makes a good dipping sauce for lamb riblets served as appetizers.

8 cups blackberries, rinsed and drained
1¾ cups red wine vinegar
1 cup firmly packed brown sugar
1 cup granulated sugar
2 teaspoons ground cinnamon
1½ teaspoons ground allspice
1 teaspoon ground ginger
1/2 teaspoon black pepper
2 dashes cayenne pepper (or more to taste)

Heat berries over medium-high heat in a 4 to 5 quart pan stirring often until they get juicy and begin to fall apart, about 10 minutes. Rub berries and juice through a fine strainer into a bowl; discard seeds. Return berry juice to pan and add vinegar, brown sugar, granulated sugar, cinnamon, allspice, ginger, pepper and cayenne. Bring mixture to a boil over high heat. Reduce heat and simmer gently, uncovered and stirring often until berry catsup is reduced to 2½ cups. Cool catsup and serve or chill air-tight up to 2 weeks. Freeze to store longer.

CRANBERRY ORANGE RELISH

This easy recipe from Peg Bracken's, The I Hate to Cook Book quickly became a favorite on holiday tables.

4 cups raw fresh cranberries
1 orange, quartered
1½ cups sugar

Blend ingredients in food processor. Store in covered jars in refrigerator.

STRAWBERRY FREEZER JAM
SYLVIA PESTONI

Easy and always fresh tasting.

4 cups strawberries, stemmed and washed
1/4 cup lemon juice
1 package powdered pectin
1 cup light corn syrup
5½ cups sugar

Combine and mix berries and lemon juice in a large kettle. Add pectin, stirring vigorously, allow to stand 10 minutes, stirring occasionally. Add corn syrup and mix well. Gradually stir in sugar while warming jam to 100° on a candy thermometer. Do not heat above 100°. When sugar is dissolved, ladle into pint jars, leaving 1" headroom at top and freeze at once. After initial freezing jam will keep in refrigerator for several weeks. It will keep in freezer for a year. Makes 4 pints.

GREEN TOMATO RELISH
BEV POPKO

8 green tomatoes, thinly sliced
2¾ pounds onions, thinly sliced
1/2 cup salt
1½ quarts cider vinegar
2 pounds brown sugar
2 pounds green bell peppers, sliced
1 pound red bell peppers, diced
6 cloves garlic, minced
t tablespoon dry mustard
1½ teaspoons salt

SPICE BAG -TIE IN MOIST CLOTH
1 tablespoon whole cloves
1 tablespoon ground ginger
1½ teaspoons celery seeds
3" cinnamon stick, broken

Combine tomatoes, onions and 1/2 cup salt in large bowl. Stir well, cover and refrigerate 12 hours. Rinse in cold water and drain. Use a non-reactive pan for cooking. Combine tomatoes, onions and other ingredients. Mix well, add spice bag with herbs and cook, stirring often until tomatoes are translucent, about 1 hour. Remove spice bag and can while hot or cool and refrigerate for up to 1 month. About 6 pint jars.

Eating in St. Helena

TOMATILLO SAUCE
BILL YOUNG

A note regarding tomatillos. There are two types - green and purple. Both can be used in this recipe. The purple is said to have more flavor. If tomatillos are fresh picked they can be sun dried in their huskes to improve flavor. When making this the first time I failed to put the lid on the blender. As a result I spent more time cleaning the kitchen than I did making the sauce.

8 cups tomatillos, husked, washed, and each cut in half or thirds
1/4 cup canola oil
1 cup diced white onion
10 cloves garlic, diced
2 cups chicken broth
2 teaspoons ground cumin
1 tablespoon Italian seasoning or oregano leaves
3 tablespoons lime juice
2 tablespoons sugar
6-8 hot chili peppers - jalapeno, arbolo - whole

Sauté onions in oil in a large pan until almost-translucent. Add garlic and cook until onions are translucent, about 10 minutes. Add tomatillos, chicken broth, seasonings, lime juice and sugar. Add whole chili peppers. Reduce heat to medium and bring to boil, stirring frequently. Reduce heat and simmer 30 minutes, stirring occassionally. Remove whole chilies and set them aside. Divide sauce into two equal parts. Put one half into blender and add two hot peppers after slicing them. Do not remove skin or seeds of hot peppers. Process until desired consistancy. Sample and decide if you need more hot peppers. Repeat the process with remaining sauce. Add more peppers for a hotter sauce. By doing this in two batches you can have a hot and a mild version.

GAME SAUCE
MARY ANN MC COMBER

We ate a lot of game meat. I often served these delicious meats with the following sauce.

1 part current jelly
1 part butter
1 part Worcestershire Sauce
1 part lemon juice

Mix together and heat until butter and jelly are melted.

MINT SAUCE
SANDY HERRICK

This recipe comes from Lake Creek Lodge in Sisters, Oregon.

4 cups brown sugar
1/2 cup lemon juice
1 cup apple cider vinegar
dash salt
1 cup finely chopped mint

Mix brown sugar, lemon juice, vinegar and salt. Heat until slightly thickened. Add mint. Serve warm on lamb.

SUGARED BACON STRIPS
VALERIE PRESTEN

From United Airlines in-flight Mainliner magazine, January 1975, originally from golfer Arnold Palmer. Obviously written before plastic grocery bags - see directions for draining bacon. Easy and delicious.

1 pound bacon
1 cup brown sugar

Bring bacon to room temperature. Sprinkle strips with brown sugar and pat in on both sides. Place strips on a flat pan with sides and bake in 300°-350° oven 20-30 minutes until they are dark brown. Turn over once. Remove with tongs and throughly drain on brown paper. (Grocery bags are excellent.) As bacon cools it will get hard and can be broken into pieces or served whole.

MUSTARD GRAVY OR SAUCE
SANDY HERRICK

1 cup Guldens' mustard
1 cup sugar
1 cup white vinegar
1 cup Campbell's tomato soup, undiluted
1 cup melted butter
1 teaspoon salt
3 egg yolks, beaten

Mix ingredients and cook slowly over medium heat until mixture thickens slightly. Great on ham. Serve hot as a gravy or cold as a spread for sandwiches. Keeps for weeks in refrigerator or can be frozen.

APRICOT CHUTNEY
PHOEBE ELLSWORTH

My mother made Apricot Chutney every year for gifts to friends. Also to serve at home with chicken, lamb or as an hors d'oeuvre over cream cheese. I do the same. If you happen to pick an especially hot spell for chutney making, assemble all ingredients except raisins and currents the night before cooking. Cook in the morning when it's cooler.

**5 pounds apricots, pitted and cut into
  small pieces
2 pounds brown sugar
1 quart cider vinegar
2 pounds red onions, chopped
2 oranges ground in food processor
4 teaspoons mustard seeds
2 teaspoons tumeric
2 teaspoons chili powder
1 teaspoon cinnamon
1 teaspoon cloves
1/2 cup fresh grated ginger root
2 pounds golden raisins
1 pound dried currents**

Assemble all ingredients except raisins and currents in large heavy kettle. Bring to boil slowly and cook about 60 minutes. Stir frequently as chutney can burn bottom of pan quickly. Add raisins and currents after first hour of cooking. Cook 30 minutes more. Pack in sterile canning jars when hot – seal. Chutney is better if aged a couple of months before eating.

MEYER LEMON RELISH
SARAH GALBRAITH

Excellent with most fish. Use Meyer lemons only.

**1 shallot finely diced, or substitute red onion
1 tablespoon lemon juice
salt to taste
2 small Meyer lemons
1/2 cup extra-virgin olive oil
sugar to taste**

Combine shallots, lemon juice and salt. Let stand 15 minuts. Cut each lemon into 8 wedges. Discard center core and seeds. Chop off ends. Slice wedges into thin slivers. Comine with shallots and stir in olive oil. Add sugar to taste.

GERMAINE SAUCE
MARCIA MAHER

The Maher Family sent us this savory recipe from Marcia's recipe collection. Shannon's notes said it's a gorgeous green color that looks great over salmon or other fish.

**1 bunch scallions, chopped
1/2 teaspoon minced ginger
1 bunch fresh dill, chopped
1/4 cup lemon juice
1/4 cup soy sauce
1/2 teaspoon sugar
1/4 cup canola or grape seed oil**

EASY WAY
Put all ingredients in blender and blend until smooth.
MARCIA'S WAY
Skillfully chop onions, ginger and herbs. Mix lemon juice, sugar and soy sauce in bowl until sugar has dissolved then wisk in oil. Mix in onions, ginger and herbs and serve over perfectly grilled fish.

MOM MORGAN'S MUSTARD PICKLES
DONNA MORGAN

This is a large recipe and perfect for Christmas gifting.

4½ quarts cucumbers, cut into small chunks
1 quart cauliflower flowerets (small)
1 quart pickling onions
1 pint water
1½ quarts cider vinegar
1 package mixed pickling spices
Mix thoroughly together:
1 cup flour
1 tablespoon tumeric
2 teaspoons celery seed
6 tablespoons Colman's dry mustard
2 cups white vinegar
1 pound brown sugar
1 small jar French's prepared mustard
1 pint bottle Cross & Blackwell mustard pickles

Put 3 tablespoons salt over cucumbers, cover with boiling water and let them come to a boil. Immediately pour off boiling water to let cucumbers cool. Steam cauliflower only until crisp-tender. Cool. Bring vinegar and water to boil and add package of spices placed in a cheesecloth bag. Let steep for a few minutes. Add onions and cook until opaque. Whisk dry ingredients into vinegar solution. Boil for approximately 4 minutes. Add one small bottle French's prepared mustard and one pint bottle Crosse & Blackwell mustard pickles. Let come to a boil and bottle.

MYSTERIOUS MARVELOUS MUSTARD
PHOEBE ELLSWORTH

The person who first gave me this recipe swore me to secrecy. When I found the identical recipe in The San Francisco Junior League Cookbook, I decided it was okay to let the cat out of the bag. Wonderful with an Easter ham.

1 cup Colman's dry mustard
1 cup cider vinegar
1 cup sugar (brown is best)
4 eggs, lightly beaten

Soak dry mustard in vinegar overnight. Place in top of double boiler and add sugar and eggs. Cook slowly, stirring constantly, for about 10 minuetes or until thick. If you are not going to use all of this in a few days, place in sterilized jars and store in refrigerator for up to 3 months. Add fresh herbs or use herb-flavored vinegar for variety. Makes 1½ pints.

Eating in St. Helena

PESTO
SYLVIA PESTONI AND PHOEBE ELLSWORTH
FROM MARY MAGGETTI

Mary lived between us on Tainter Street in the early 70's. She gave us many cooking tips. Pesto can be frozen and doing so in an ice-cube tray makers handy pesto cubes to use in many dishes. If freezing, add nuts and cheese after thawing. Use pesto on pasta, soups, stews, bread or in vegetable lasagne.

2 cups loosly packed freshly basil leaves
1/2 cup pine nuts
2 cloves garlic, peeled
1/2 cup grated Parmesan cheese
1/2 cup extra-virgin olive oil
salt and pepper to taste

Place basil, nuts, garlic and cheese in food processor and grind to a thick paste. with machine running, slowly pour oil into mixture. If sauce seems dry, add a little more oil. Add salt and pepper. Use immediately or store in covered glass jar in refrigerator up to 1 week or freeze. Above amount enough for 1 pound pasta.

PARSLEY PESTO
SYLVIA PESTONI

Delicous on French bread, tomatoes and more.

1 packed cup fresh parsley
1/4 cup snipped chives
1 clove garlic
1/3 to 1/2 cup olive oil
salt and pepper to taste.

Process in food processor as in above pesto recipe.

Desserts

*The only way to get rid of temptation
is to yield to it.*
Oscar Wilde

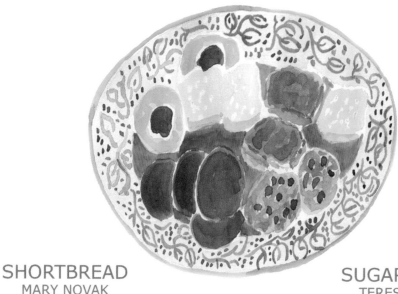

SHORTBREAD
MARY NOVAK

This recipe came to me from Judy Newman.

1/2 pound butter
1 cup sugar
1 teaspoon vanilla
3 cups flour

Blend in Cuisinart in 2 batches. Press into pan and score. Bake 325° 40 minutes or until done.

LEMON BARS
VERA HAMPTON

2 cups sifted flour
1/2 cup sifted powdered sugar
2 cubes butter, cut into small pieces
4 eggs
2 cups sugar
1/3 CUP lemon juice
1/4 cup flour
1/2 teaspoon baking powder

CRUST
Mix 2 cups flour, powdered sugar and butter until well-blended and crumbly. Press into 9" x 12" baking pan. Bake 350° 25 minutes.
FILLING
Beat eggs, 2 cups sugar and lemon juice until fluffy. Add 1/4 cup flour and baking soda. Pour over baked crust. Bake 350° 25 minutes or longer, until set in center. Sprinkle with powdered sugar. Cool and cut.

SUGAR COOKIES
TERESE PARRIOTT

1 cup margarine
1 cup Crisco oil
1 cup sugar
1 cup powdered sugar
1 teaspoon salt
2 eggs
4 cups flour
1 teaspoon baking soda
1 teaspoon cream of tarter
1 teaspoon vanilla

Cream margarine, oil and both sugars. Add eggs and beat 2 minutes. Sift flour, soda, salt and cream of tarter together and add to creamed mixture. Beat until blended. Add vanilla and mix. Chill in refrigerator for at least 2 hours. Make balls about the size of large walnuts. Flatten with bottom of glass dipped in sugar. (I dip glass in sugar before pressing each cookie.) Use ungreased cookie sheet. Bake 350° 15 minutes.

NANCY'S CHUNKY CHOCOLATE CHIP COOKIES
SHERLYN ZUMWALT

This recipe is a favorite of Allison's. She spent a good amount of time at the Cunningham's with her friend Laura and they made these cookies a lot. At the end of the recipe, which she copied, she added "Yummy!"

1 box German Chocolate cake mix
6 ounce package semi sweet
chocolate chips
1/2 cup cooking oil
2 eggs

Mix together and bake on un-greased pan. Bake 325° 8-10 minutes.

Eating in St. Helena

PERSIMMON COOKIES
SHIRLEY SPARKS FROM BERNICE SCHEIBAL

From 1445 Oak Avenue persimmons.

1 cup sugar
1/2 cup shortening
1 egg, beaten
1 teaspoon soda
1 cup persimmon pulp
2 cups all purpose flour
1/2 teaspoon salt
2 teaspoons cloves
1 teaspoon cinnamon
1/2 teaspoon nutmeg
1 cup raisins
1 cup chopped walnuts

Cream sugar and shortening, add beaten egg. Add soda to persimmon pulp and combine with sugar mixture. Sift dry ingredients and mix in raisins and walnuts. Combine with other mixture. Drop by teaspoonsful onto greased cookie sheet. Bake 350° 10-15 minutes. Makes about 3 dozen cookies.

LEMON GLAZED PERSIMMON BARS
CAROLYN PRIDE

1 cup persimmon pulp, fresh
1½ teaspoons lemon juice
1 teaspoon baking soda
1 egg
1 cup sugar
1/2 cup vegetable oil
8 ounces dates, chopped
1¾ cups flour
1 teaspoon cinnamon
1 teaspoon nutmeg
1/4 teaspoon ground cloves
1 cup chopped nuts
1 cup powdered sugar
4 tablespoons lemon juice

Mix persimmon pulp, lemon juice, baking soda; set aside. Lightly beat egg, stir in sugar, oil and dates. Combine flour and spices; add to date mixture just until blended. Spread in greased and floured jelly roll pan 10" x 15". Bake 350° about 25 minutes until lightly browned. Cool in pan on rack 5 minutes. Spread with lemon glaze, cool thoroughly, and then cut into bars. Keep well wrapped.
LEMON GLAZE: Blend one cup un-sifted powdered sugar with 4 tablespoons lemon juice until smooth.

OATMEAL FUDGE BARS
MARY NOVAK

Very Good!!

OATMEAL LAYER
1/2 cup shortening or butter
1 cup light brown sugar, packed
1 egg
1/2 teaspoon vanilla
3/4 cup flour
1/2 teaspoon soda
1/2 teaspoon salt
2 cups oatmeal
1/2 cup chopped walnuts

Cream shortening and sugar. Add egg and vanilla. Sift flour with baking powder and salt and add to mixture. Mix in oatmeal. Reserve one cup for topping. Press rest of mixture in greased 9" x 9" pan.
FUDGE LAYER
1 6 ounce package chocolate chips
1 tablespoon butter
1/3 cup sweet condensed milk
1/4 teaspoon salt
1 teaspoon vanilla
1/2 cup chopped walnuts

Combine chocolate chips, butter, milk and salt and melt in small saucepan. Remove from heat, add vanilla and nuts. Spread over oatmeal layer. Sprinkle top with reserved oatmeal mixture. Bake 350° 25 minutes. Recipe easily doubled for 9" X 13" or 10" x 14" pan.

MAMMIE'S BROWNIES
SUSAN SMITH

Fattening, but good because of the almond extract.

4 squares of bittersweet chocolate
1/2 cup oil
2 cups sugar
4 eggs
1 teaspoon almond extract
1 cup flour

Preheat oven to 350°. Grease a 9" x 9" pan. Melt chocolate in microwave in a medium sized bowl. Blend in oil and sugar. Add eggs and almond extract. Mix in flour. Bake 20 minutes.

Eating in St. Helena

CHOCOLATE SHORTBREAD
ANN PUTNAM

2 cups all purpose flour
1 cup powdered sugar
1/2 to 1 cup strained Dutch process cocoa
1/4 teaspoon kosher salt or
1/8 teaspoon sea salt
2 cubes butter, cold, unsalted
1 teaspoon vanilla

Preheat oven to 300°. Pour all dry ingredients into food processor, pulse to mix well. (If an electric mixer is used butter should be creamed with sugar and vanilla first.) Add cold butter and vanilla. Process until a shiny dough forms and gathers to one side of the processor bowl. Quickly remove dough and wrap in plastic wrap, pressing to form a thick disc. Keep dough cold in the refrigerator until you are ready to roll it out. If it has gotten stiff, let it warm a bit but not too much or it will stick to the rolling pin. Before rolling dough out, flour a pastry cloth or a wood surface and place dough on the surface. Flour rolling pin, also. Roll dough to 1/2" thickness. Dough may be rolled to 1/4" thick but you must adjust baking time, so as not to over bake. Cut cookies with cookie cutter of your choice. A simple shape works best.

Place cookies on parchment placed on a heavy cookie sheet. If not baking right away put sheet of cookies in refrigerator to stay cool. Adjust 2 oven baking racks to divide oven into thirds or bake in the middle if you only have one cookie sheet full of cookies.

Place sheet or sheets in oven. If using lower temperature, bake longer. Chocolate should not be baked at too high a heat or for too long. When you begin to smell chocolate, check cookies – about 20 minutes. They should be soft on top but dry enough to touch. Let sit out of oven for a few minutes to cool a bit, then move with a spatula to a baking rack to cool completely. These freeze well, but are a bit fragile, especially if under baked.

PUMPKIN COOKIES
SYLVIA PESTONI

Sylvia and family had a pumpkin patch on White-hall Lane from 1976-1987. Everyone in the family helped and they were open the last two weeks of October. Schools from all over Napa County brought second graders to the patch. Friends helped to make pumpkin cookies and pumpkin bread.

1 cup butter, softened
1/2 cup honey
1/4 cup brown sugar
2 eggs, well beaten
2 cups pumpkin puree
1 teaspoon baking soda
2 teaspoons baking powder
1½ teaspoons cinnamon
1 teaspoon allspice
1/2 teaspoon salt
2 cups whole-wheat flour
1/2 cup wheat germ or more flour
1/2 cup chopped nuts - walnuts, pecans, etc.
1/2 cup raisins

Preheat oven to 350°. Slowly add sugar to butter, creaming until light. Mix in well-beaten eggs, honey and pumpkin. Combine and sift flour, wheat germ, baking powder, baking soda and seasonings and add to pumpkin mixture. Stir in raisins and chopped nuts. Mix until well blended. Drop batter by teaspoonsful onto buttered cookie sheet and flatten with fork. Bake 18 minutes or until light brown. Makes about 6 dozen. May be frozen.

MURIEL'S GUMDROP COOKIES
PAULA YOUNG

This was our family's favorite recipe from my aunt. Muriel. She taught in the Seattle Public Schools for many years and she loved to bake. This is a bar cookie.

3 eggs
2 cups brown sugar
1/4 cup canned milk
2 cups flour
1/2 teaspoon salt
1 teaspoon cinnamon
1 cup cut-up gum drops
1/2 cup chopped nuts

Beat eggs, brown sugar and milk together. Sift flour, salt and cinnamon and add to egg mixture. Add gum drops and nuts. Bake in a shallow pan. 350° 35 minutes.

RUTHIE'S FAVORITE COOKIES
MARY NOVAK

1 can Eagle Brand condensed milk
1 6 ounce package chocolate chips
1 cup walnuts, chopped
18 graham crackers

Roll graham crackers into crumbs. Mix with other ingredients. Place in 9" X 9" pan. Bake 350° 25 minutes. Cool and cut into squares.

Eating in St. Helena

ISABELLE'S RAISIN FILLED COOKIES
DONNA MORGAN

When I was growing up on a Montana ranch my mother's kitchen was the place, neighbors, family and drop-ins gathered because of what Isabelle would pull from her oven on a daily basis. Although the holiday season brought smells of cinnamon and ginger, the smell of her buttery raisin filled cookies coming out of the oven surpassed all others and to this day remain my favorite Christmas cookie. Santa does not come to our house until these are mellowing in their tightly sealed container. This is not a recipe for the faint hearted. Several time consuming steps are involved but it is well worth the effort.

3/4 cup butter
1 cup sugar
2 eggs
3 teaspoons baking powder
1/2 cup milk
3½ cups flour (approximate)

Cream butter, add sugar, beat until creamy. Add eggs. Beat. Add milk. Beat. Add flour and baking powder. Roll thin. Cut with cookie cutter. Spread filling in center then top with second layer of dough and seal edges by pressing with finger tip. I inherited the antique Spam can with which Mother cut her cookies. Trust me. You can use a round cutter, but the Spam can is what makes all the difference.

FILLING
1 cup ground raisins
1 cup sugar mixed with 2 tablespoons flour
1/2 cup water
juice and grated rind of 1 lemon or more if you like
Cook until thick. Cool.

BUTTERY PECAN COOKIES
SUSAN EDELEN

Susan makes these goodies for her bridge friends at Christmas time.

2 cubes butter
3/4 cup brown sugar, packed
1 large egg yolk
1 cup all-purpose flour
1/2 teaspoon salt
1 cup chopped pecans
pecan half pieces

Preheat oven to 325°. Cream butter, sugar and egg yolk. Add flour, salt, chopped pecans. Drop batter by teaspoonsful on greased cookie sheet. Press pecan half in center. Bake 12-15 minutes. Makes 3 dozen delicious cookies.

STEAMED PERSIMMON PUDDING
KAREN DAHL

1 cup persimmon puree (about 3 persimmons)
2 teaspoons baking soda
1 cube butter, room temperature
1 cup sugar
2 eggs
1 tablespoon fresh lemon juice
1 tablespoon rum
1 cup all purpose flour
1 teaspoon cinnamon
1/2 teaspoon salt
1 cup chopped walnut or pecan pieces
1 cup raisins
LEMON SAUCE
1/4 cube butter
1/2 cup cream
1/3 cup sugar
juice of 1 lemon

Put persimmon puree in a small bowl and stir in baking soda. Set aside. Cream butter and sugar together. Add eggs, lemon juice and rum. Beat well. Add flour, cinnamon and salt. Stir to blend. Add persimmon puree and beat until well mixed. Stir in nuts and raisins. Spoon batter into a prepared mold (greased 2 quart pudding mold with a lid). Cover tightly. Place mold on a rack in a large stock pot or Dutch oven which is filled with boiling water (enough to come halfway up the sides of the mold). Allow pudding to steam about 2 hours, on stove top. Remove mold from pot and set aside for 5 minutes. Turn out pudding onto a rack. Serve warm or at room temperature, with softly whipped cream or lemon sauce.
LEMON SAUCE
Boil butter, sugar and cream for 5 minutes. Add juice of 1 lemon.

MYSTERY PUDDING
SHIRLEY SPARKS
FROM HER MOTHER, BERNICE SCHEIBAL

1 cup sifted flour
1 teaspoon baking soda
1/4 teaspoon salt
1 egg
2/3 cup sugar
1 teaspoon vanilla
1 can fruit cocktail
1/4 cup packed brown sugar
1/2 teaspoon cinnamon
1/2 cup chopped nuts
1/2 pint whipping cream for topping

Sift flour, baking soda and salt. In a small bowl, beat egg and sugar together; add vanilla, fruit cocktail (syrup and all). Stir in flour mixture. Mix in brown sugar and cinnamon. Pour into small casserole or 8" x 8" pan. Sprinkle nuts on top. Bake 350° 40–50 minutes. Spoon in bowls and top with whipped cream.

Eating in St. Helena

PAVLOVA
MARIANNE PETERSEN

Don't make Pavlova if it's raining – meringue doesn't stay crisp in humidity. Easy and festive.

4 egg whites, room temperature
pinch salt
1/2 cup sugar
1/2 teaspoon vanilla
1 teaspoon white vinegar
1 level tablespoon cornstarch
1/2 pint whipping cream
berries or other fresh fruit

Beat egg whites with pinch of salt for 5 or 6 minutes, gradually adding sugar, vinegar and vanilla. Beat until stiff. Sift cornstarch and fold in lightly. Wet large oven-proof plate and heap mixture in middle of the damp surface.
GAS OVEN 400° 10 minutes, reduce heat to 250° bake 60 minutes more.
ELECTRIC OVEN Preheat to 400°. Pace Pavlova in oven and immediately reduce heat to 250° bake undisturbed no longer than 90 minutes. Cool and top with whipped cream and decorate plate with berries or other fruit.

ARROZ CON LECHE
SYLVIA CENDEJAS

3 cups water
1/2 cinnamon stick
1 cup rice
5 cups fat free milk
1 teaspoon vanilla
1 can La Lechera condensed milk

Boil water with cinnamon stick. When boiling add rice and boil 10-15 minutes until rice is soft. Add 5 cups fat free milk and vanilla. Let rice boil 30 minutes. Add condensed milk. Rice should be boiling at mid temperature until most of milk is evaporated. Stir constantly so rice won't stick to pan. This will take 1-2 hours. Serve hot or chilled. Serves 3.

Eating in St. Helena

PAVLOVA
BARBARA SHAFER

6 egg whites, room temperature
1 2/3 cups sugar
1/4 teaspoon salt
2 teaspoons white vinegar
2 teaspoons vanilla
1 tablespoon cornstarch
1/4 cup boiling water
1 pint whipping cream
berries or other fresh fruit

Preheat oven to 375°. Beat all ingredients for 20 minutes or until stiff peaks form. Mixture should be glossy. Place in mound on foil lined baking sheet. Bake 375° 10 minutes. Reduce heat to 250°. Bake approximately 2 hours more. Cool with oven door ajar. When cooled, top with whipped cream and fruit.

RICE PUDDING
SUSAN SMITH

This has always been a Smith family favorite – delicious and nutritious. Easily doubled or tripled.

1 cup water
1/2 cup rice
4 cups milk
1/4 cup butter
3 eggs, beaten
1/2 cup sugar
1/2 teaspoon vanilla
raisins soaked in brandy, optional
cinnamon

Bring water to a boil then add rice and cover. Cook exactly 7 minutes until water is absorbed. Add milk and butter. Bring to a slow simmer, stirring occasionally. Be careful not to let bottom of pan burn. When mixture is thick (45 – 60 minutes depending on flame height) add eggs that have been beaten with sugar. Remove from heat and stir in vanilla. Add raisins, if desired. Let cool. Sprinkle some sugar mixed with cinnamon over all and serve.

FAIRY PIE
PATTY VASCONI

Hap's favorite from his mother Gertrude. She was featured with this recipe in The Napa Register in 1938.

1/2 cup sugar
4 egg yolks
1 rounded teaspoon baking powder
1/4 cup milk
1/2 cup shortening
3/4 cup cake flower
4 egg whites
1 cup granulated sugar
1 teaspoon vanilla
1/2 cup finely chopped walnuts
1/2 pint whipping cream
bananas, sliced or other fresh fruit

Cream shortening, 1/2 cup sugar and egg yolks. Sift baking powder and flour. Add alternately with milk. Spread evenly in 2 9" cake pans and refrigerate 60 minutes. Whip egg whites with 1 cup sugar and vanilla. Spread on cakes and sprinkle with walnuts. Bake 325° 20-25 minutes. Cool. Place one cake, nut side down on plate. Cover with whipped cream and bananas or other fruit. Place other layer, nut side up on top.

ANGEL PIE
MARIE DEL BONDIO

Very popular dessert - everybody served it at showers and luncheons. Do not make when it's raining.

4 egg whites
1 cup sugar
1 teaspoon cream of tarter

Beat together with fury. Line a pie pan with mixture making a nest in the center. Bake 350° 60 minutes.

CUSTARD
4 egg yolks
1/2 cup sugar
lemon juice
zemon zest

Cook in double boiler, beating and stirring until thick. Pour in the egg white shell. Let sit 24 hours before serving. Top with whipped cream and lemon zest or candied lemon.

NUT TORTE
WILLINDA MCCREA

Here is a recipe Peter and I inherited from his mom, Eleanor, which goes back at least to the early 60's when we first served it. It's easy and guys always ask for seconds.

3 egg whites
1 cup sugar
1 cup crushed graham crackers
1 cup finely chopped walnuts or pecans
apricot or raspberry jam
whipped cream

Beat egg whites. Add sugar and beat again. Stir in crushed graham crackers and finely chopped nuts. Place in well-greased pie plate. Bake 350° 30 minutes. Cool and top with apricot or raspberry jam and whipped cream.

CHOCOLATE PEANUT BUTTER PIE
CAROLE PARR

We were vacationing in Natchez, Mississippi and had this for dessert at The Post House. Later on I wrote them and they graciously sent me the recipe. It's to die for.

3 cups milk
1¼ cups sugar
1/3 cup cocoa
1/3 cup cornstarch
1/4 teaspoon salt
1½ teaspoons vanilla
3 tablespoons butter
1 pie shell, baked
1/2 cup peanut butter
1 cup confectioners sugar
1/2 pint whipping cream

Combine cocoa, sugar and cornstarch in a pan. Blend in milk until smoooth. Cook over medium heat. Boil and stir about 3 minutes. Remove from heat, add butter and vanilla. Mix peanut butter and 1 cup confectioners sugar until mealy. Line baked pie shell with peanut butter mixture. Save some to sprinkle on top. Cover with chocolate mixture, then whipped cream. Sprinkle peanut butter mixture on top of whipped cream.

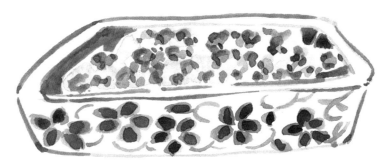

GRASSHOPPER PIE
HELEN GHIRINGHELLI NELSON

My mom loved Grasshopper Pie.

14 Oreo or Hydrox cookies
3 tablespoons butter, melted
3 tablespoons white crème de cocoa
4 tablespoons crème de menthe
24 marshmallows
1/2 cup milk
1/2 pint whipped cream

Roll and crush cookies. Mix with melted butter and press into pie pan. In a double boiler melt marshmallows and milk. Add crème de cocoa and crème de menthe. Cool. Fold in whipped cream. Pour into pie shell. Sprinkle with cookie crumbs. Refrigerate until ready to serve.

PEACH AND RASBERRY COBBLER
LORAINE STUART

9 peaches - about 3 pounds
1 cup sugar
1 teaspoon salt
2 tablespoons cornstarch
2 tablespoons lemon juice
1 pint rasberries
1½ cups flour
1½ teaspoons baking powder
3/4 tablespoon salt
5 tablespoons butter, chilled
2/3 cup milk

Preheat oven to 400°. Peel and slice peaches. Combine them with 3/4 cup sugar, cornstarch and lemon juice. Gently stir in rasberries. Transfer to 2 quart baking dish. Cover with foil. Bake until juices are bubbling, about 30 minutes.

Combine 1/4 cup sugar, flour, baking powder and salt. Cut in butter until mixture resembles coarse meal. Stir milk into flour mixture until ingredients just hold together. Drop 8 heaping spoonsful of dough onto hot fruit and sprinkle remaining sugar on dough. Bake uncovered until biscuits have browned, about 25 minutes.

APPLE CRISP
LOIS SWANSON

One of the best apple crisp recipes I have ever-tasted and I have tried many.

4 cups baking apples, pared, sliced & cored (about 6 medium)
3/4 cup brown sugar, packed
1/2 cup all-purpose flour
1/2 cup rolled oats
3/4 teaspoon cinnamon
3/4 teaspoon nutmeg
1/3 cup butter, soft
whipped cream or ice cream

Preheat oven to 375°. Place sliced apples in greased 8" x 8" pan. Blend remaining ingredients until mixture is crumbly. Spread over apples. Bake 30-35 minutes, or until apples are tender and topping is golden brown. Serve warm with cream or ice cream.

MOCK APPLE PIE
HELEN GHIRINGHELLI NELSON

I fooled the neighbors with Mock Apple Pie. They thought it was real apples.

pastry for a 2 crust 9" pie

36 round cheese crackers
2 cups sugar
2 cups water
2 teaspoons cream of tartar
1 teaspoon lemon peel, shredded
2 tablespoons lemon juice
2 tablespoons butter
3/4 teaspoon cinnamon

Roll out pastry for bottom crust and fit into a 9" pie pan. Carefully break crackers into the pastry lined pie pan. In a sauce-pan combine sugar, water and cream of tartar. Bring to boiling and boil gently uncovered for 15 minutes. Remove from heat. Add lemon peel and lemon juice. Cool. Pour syrup over crackers. Dot with butter and sprinkle with cinnamon. Cover with top crust and cut with slits. Bake 425° 10-35 minutes until crust is golden. Serve warm.

PEAR OR PEACH (FREESTONE) GLAZED PIE
SUE FOGARTY

This was Jim's mother's recipe. I am not a baker, but did learn to do this, as pear pie was one of Jim's favorites. I found that heaping the fruit high was best as it cooks down. Bake on a cookie sheet as this pie drips out.

3/4 cup sugar
1/3 cup flour
1/4 cup butter
sliced pears or peeled peaches
1 unbaked pie shell

Blend sugar, flour and butter to a crumble. Alternate mixture with fruit in unbaked pie shell. Bake 350° 60-70 minutes.

PEAR PIE
BARBARA SHURTZ

Pear pie is a fairly new recipe but it is very good and so easy to make. The original directions were to use a frozen, store bought pie shell, something I had never done until I discovered this recipe. I must have made hundreds of wine cakes for fund raisers or pot lucks because they, too, are so easy and so good by themselves or with fruit on the side.

4 or more pears, sliced
1/2 cube butter, soft
1 cup sugar
4 tablespoons flour
1 teaspoon vanilla
2 eggs
1 unbaked pie shell

Place cut pears into unbaked pie shell. Cream together all other ingredients and pour over pears. Bake at 350° 85 minutes.

PUMPKIN CHIFFON PIE
BARBARA RYAN

9" baked pie shell
1 tablespoon gelatin
1/4 cup water, cold
3 eggs, separated
1/3 cup sugar
1¼ cups canned pumpkin
1/2 cup milk
3/4 teaspoon cinnamon
3/4 teaspoon nutmeg

Soak gelatin in cold water. Slightly beat egg yolks and add sugar, canned pumpkin, milk, cinnamon and nutmeg. Cook and stir over hot, not boiling, water until dissolved. Chill. Whip egg whites until stiff but not dry and fold into mixture. When pumpkin mixture begins to set, stir in sugar and whipped cream.

PUMPKIN AND ICE CREAM PIE
ANN CARPY

1 pumpkin
Preheat oven to 325°. Cut pumpkin in half, remove seeds and strings. Place on cookie sheet, cut side down. Bake until soft.

1 cup ginger snap cookie crumbs
1/4 cup sugar
1/4 cup butter
1 cup fresh pumpkin, cooked and mashed
1/3 cup brown sugar
1 teaspoon pumpkin pie spice
1 quart vanilla ice cream
1/2 cup chopped nuts mixed with some of the cookie crumbs
1/2 pint whipping cream

Mix crumbs with granulated sugar and butter. Press into bottom of a pie pan. Blend pumpkin with brown sugar and spices. Fold pumpkin into ice cream. Pour into prepared crust and freeze until firm. Cut into wedges and top with whipped cream and nuts.
NOTE For easy cutting, remove pie from oven 20 minutes prior to serving

Eating in St. Helena

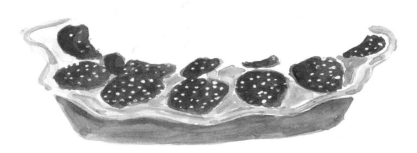

STRAWBERRY PIE
SUE CROSS

A "pig-out" pie!

1½ cups flour
1/2 cup shortening
1/4 teaspoon salt
3½ tablespoons ice water
2 baskets strawberries, mashed
1 basket strawberries, whole
1/2 cup water
1 cup sugar
3 tablespoons cornstarch
1/2 pint whipping cream

Blend flour, shortening, salt and ice water. Roll out to fit pie pan. Bake 325° 10-15 minutes. Add 1/2 cup water, sugar and cornstarch to mashed berries. Cook on medium heat stirring all the time – simmer for 2 minutes. Place reserved berries, points up, in cooled pie crust and pour cooled berry mixture over all. Top with whipped cream.

CHOCOLATE PECAN PIE
KATA BROWNELL

We eat simpler meals now. Here is a "killer" recipe from the past. I figured it out for myself after having it in a restaurant in Humboldt County. (They refused to give me the recipe.) It is the most called for one that kids, grandkids and friends request.

1½ cups dark corn syrup
4 cubes semi-sweet chocolate, melted
1 tablespoon butter, melted and cooled
1 teaspoon vanilla extract
1 9" partially baked short-crust pastry shell
1½ cups halved pecans, (about 6 ounces)

Preheat oven to 400°. With a wire whisk, rotary or electric beater, beat eggs in a mixing bowl for about 30 seconds or until they are smooth. Beating constantly, pour in corn syrup in a slow, thin stream. Add cooled melted butter, melted chocolate and vanilla. Continue to beat until all ingredients are well blended. Pour into pie shell and scatter pecan halves evenly over the top. Bake 35 minutes until filling is firm to the touch. Serve warm or at room temperature.

COCONUT PIE
MARIE OLIVER

This is the best thing I make and I do a lot of cooking. It is not for the sophisticate, but even they think it is good. It is very Southern.

1 cup sugar
1 can Angel Flake coconut
3 eggs
2 teaspoons flour
1/2 cube butter, softened
1 cup milk
1 teaspoon vanilla
1 pie crust, unbaked

Sprinkle 2 to 3 tablespoons coconut in bottom of pie crust. Mix all other ingredients and pour into pie crust. Bake at 350° 10 minutes, reduce oven to 300° bake 20 minutes more or until set (a little wobbly is perfect) and brown.

Eating in St. Helena

NECTARINE SURPRISE
MAYBETH EGNER

nectarines, halved
blue cheese
half and half
splash of brandy

Bring blue cheese to room temperature and mix
with small amount of half and half. Add brandy
and put nut-size spoonful in center of nectarines.

SUMMER
STRAWBERRY DELIGHT
PHOEBE ELLSWORTH

*From Emily Chase's, The Pleasures of Cooking
with Wine.*

3 oranges
1 tablespoon lemon peel, grated
grated peel from oranges
1 cup rosé wine
1/2 cup sugar
2 tablespoons cornstarch
3 pints strawberries, sliced

Grate peel from oranges. Squeeze oranges
– should be about 1 cup juice. Mix cornstarch
with small amount of juice. Add rest of juice,
wine, grated peels and sugar. Heat until clear and
slightly thickened. Cool. Pour over sliced strawberries. Cover and chill several hours to blend
flavors. Serves 8.

88

RAW CARROT CAKE
SHIRLEY SPARKS

2 cups flour
2 cups sugar
2 teaspoons soda
2 teaspoons cinnamon
dash of nutmeg
1 teaspoon salt
1¼ cups oil
4 eggs, beaten
2 cups grated raw carrots

Mix oil and sugar, then add eggs, dry ingredients and carrots. Bake at 350° 35-40 minutes in
greased and floured pans.
ICING
8 ounces cream cheese
1/2 cube butter
1 pound powdered sugar
1/2 cup coarsely chopped nuts

Mix cream cheese, butter,
powdered sugar and nuts together.

BEST CARROT PINEAPPLE CAKE
SUSAN SMITH

*I like to add raisins and walnuts myself, but some
people in our family don't like raisins.*

1½ cups brown sugar
4 eggs
1½ cups Wesson oil
2 cups flour
2 teaspoons baking soda
1 teaspoon salt
3 teaspoons cinnamon
2 cups grated raw carrots
1 cup crushed pineapple, well drained

Thoroughly mix brown sugar, eggs and oil together in a large bowl. Sift flour, soda and salt
and add to above ingredients. Add carrots and
pineapple and mix well. Oil a 9" x 13" pan, pour
in batter and bake at 350° 40 minutes. Sift powdered sugar on top when cool.

Eating in St. Helena

CHEESE CAKE
SARAH SIMPSON

21 ounces cream cheese, room temperature
3/4 cup plus 1 tablespoon sugar
1/3 cube butter, melted
2 eggs
1/4 pound graham cracker crumbs
24 ounces sour cream
1 tablespoon sugar
1 teaspoon vanilla

Preheat oven to 375°. Mix melted butter with graham cracker crumbs and press into thin layer in spring form pan. Crumble cream cheese into bowl, add eggs one at a time, beating well after each egg. Beat until creamy. Add sugar. Beat well. Pour into graham cracker crust. Bake 375° 20 minutes. Remove from oven. Carefully cover with mixture of sour cream mixed with 1 tablespoon sugar and vanilla. Return to oven and bake 5 minutes. Remove from oven and place immediately into refrigerator. After cake is well chilled, cover with plastic wrap or foil. Serve with cold fruit topping – fresh or frozen – berries, cherries, peaches, etc.

MOCHA MOUSSE CHEESECAKE
SHIRLEY SPARKS

This recipe was from Vera Hampton.

CRUST
2 cups graham cracker crumbs
1/2 cup butter
4 tablespoons sugar
1 teaspoon cinnamon
FILLING
3 8-ounce packages cream cheese
3/4 cup sugar
3 large eggs
2 semi sweet chocolate squares, German chocolate
2 tablespoons whipping cream
1 cup sour cream
1 tablespoon instant coffee, dissolved in 1/2 cup boiling water
1/4 cup coffee liqueur
2 teaspoons vanilla

Preheat oven to 350°. Beat cream cheese till smooth. Add sugar and eggs; beat at low speed till smooth. Melt chocolate and whipping cream over boiling water stirring frequently. Add to cheese mixture, blend well, and add sour cream, cooled coffee and liqueur. Turn into spring-form pan. Bake 45 minutes. Cool on rack. Refrigerate 12 hours. Top with whipped cream and shaved chocolate.

LEMON PUDDING CAKE
SUSAN SMITH

This is a nice light dessert. People my age remember this from their childhood; it must have been a recipe from the '50's. My mother used to make it. It separates during baking into a soufflé like topping with the lemon sauce underneath. Very yummy, especially when Meyer lemons are in season and available from friends' trees.

1 cup white sugar
1/4 cup flour
1/4 teaspoon salt
1/4 cup lemon juice
1 tablespoon grated lemon peel
1 tablespoon melted butter
1 cup milk
2 eggs, separated

Preheat oven to 350°. In a medium mixing bowl combine sugar, flour and salt. Stir in lemon juice, peel, butter and milk. Beat egg yolks until thick and pale and add to lemon mixture. Beat egg whites until stiff but not dry, fold into lemon mixture. Pour into a buttered 6 cup casserole. Place in a larger pan. Pour hot water to about 1" deep in the larger pan. Bake about 40 minutes, until topping is set and golden. Serve warm.

THE KEEPING ROOM MACAROON CAKE
LYNETTE BENSEN

This was a birthday cake for me many years ago and is still a favorite with my family. It freezes well and is a good traveler.

6 eggs, separated
1 cup shortening
1/2 cup butter
3 cups sugar
1/2 teaspoon almond extract
1/2 teaspoon coconut extract
3 cups cake flour, sifted
1 cup milk
7 ounces coconut

Beat yolks with shortening and butter, gradually adding sugar. Add extracts. Beat in alternately flour and milk, beginning and ending with flour. Add coconut. Beat egg whites until stiff peaks form, fold whites into batter and pour into generously greased 10" tube pan. Bake 300° 2 hours. Tester should come out clean. Cool completely before attempting to remove cake from pan. Serve with a spoon full of whipped cream, sliced strawberries or just with a dusting of powdered sugar.

ANGEL FOOD CAKE
KATHY COLLINS

Our family's favorite for birthdays. I often wondered why my mother didn't use a recipe, I now know why as I've made it for over 50 years and don't need a recipe.

2 to 1¾ cups egg whites, room temperature – about 12
1 cup sugar
1½ teaspoons cream of tartar
1½ teaspoons almond extract
1 teaspoon vanilla
1/3 teaspoon salt
1½ cups powdered sugar
1 cup cake flour
LEMON FILLING
1/2 cup lemon juice
1 can Eagle Brand condensed milk
TOP AND SIDES OF CAKE
1/2 pint whipping cream
powdered sugar
2 teaspoons almond extract
pinch salt
vanilla, a few drops

Preheat oven to 350° Beat egg whites until frothy, then add sugar a tablespoon at a time. Beat until stiff but not dry. Add cream of tartar, almond extract, vanilla and salt. Sift together powdered sugar and flour and fold into egg whites 1/4 at a time. Bake 45 to 50 minutes. Remove from oven and invert. Let cool completely in the pan.
LEMON FILLING Add lemon juice to condensed milk – it thickens up
CAKE TOP AND SIDES Whip cream, add sugar, almond extract, salt and vanilla
NOTE For chocolate angel food cake sift an additional 1/4 cup cake flour with 1/4 cup cocoa, add after sugar.

BLUMS' COFFEE CRUNCH CAKE
SYLVIA PESTONI

Blums was San Francisco's famous candy store and bakery first located at Polk and California Streets. Later they had a store in Union Square and at least one other location at the Stanford Shopping Center. This coffee crunch cake and a lemon crunch cake were birthday and other celebration favorites for years. Commuters were often asked to make a trip to Blums and people drove from all over the Bay Area to pick up one of these cakes. They were lighter than air and oh so tasty.

1 yellow sponge cake, 10" tube shape
TOPPING:
1½ cups sugar
1/4 cup strong coffee, hot
1/4 cup white corn syrup
3 teaspoons baking soda, sifted
FROSTING
1 pint whipping cream
2 tablespoons sugar
1 teaspoon vanilla

Topping may be made the day before. Measure sugar, coffee and corn syrup into a deep saucepan. Stir to mix and bring to a boil. Cook to 310° on a candy thermometer, or until a small amount dropped into cold water breaks with a snap. Remove pan from heat and stir in soda. Stir hard until mixture thickens, foams and pulls away from pan. Don't over beat. Pour immediately into an un-greased shallow pan. Do not try to stir or spread mixture. Let cool completely.
When ready to garnish cake, remove coffee mixture from pan and crush it between sheets of waxed paper until the consistency of very coarse crumbs. Split cake into four layers. Beat whipping cream with sugar and vanilla until stiff. Spread some cream between layers, then frost cake with rest of it. Cover it generously with the crushed coffee crunch, pressing lightly into cream with your fingers. Keep refrigerated. Serves 12 to 16.

Eating in St. Helena

MRS. CELLI'S AND
MRS. FORNI'S WINE CAKE
SHIRLEY SPARKS

In exchange for a dozen fresh eggs from Steve's chickens, we would have a wine cake delivered to our door by the sisters Forni and Celli. "We love to hear your chickens sing over our fence."

1 package yellow cake mix
1 package vanilla instant pudding mix
6 eggs
3/4 cup oil
1 cup Malvasia Bianca
1 teaspoon nutmeg

Combine all ingredients. Mix with electric mixer about 5 minutes at medium speed. Pour batter into a greased angel food cake pan. Bake 350° 60 minutes or until done. Cool in pan 5 minutes before turning out on a rack. Sprinkle with powdered sugar. Serves 12 to 14 people.

CAKE MIX FAVORITES
MARY ANN MC COMBER

Another memory recipe. I'd be surpised if you haven't gotten many of these. Package cake mixes came on the market before I was married in 1960. I imagine wine and rum cakes came out of the wine country.

My favorites were "lemon jello" and "white wine" cakes. I felt really talented producing those masterpieces. We took a packaged yellow cake mix, added 3 eggs, cooking oil and a box of lemon jello for the lemon jello cake. For white wine cake we used a box of white cake mix, eggs, oil, wine or port, along with a package of vanilla pudding mix. Then there was ice cream angel food cake which used a packaged angel food mix. When cooled cake is sliced in half, sideways and frosted with strawberry ice cream (summer) or mocha chocolate ice cream (winter.) It still makes my mouth water thinking about it.

Eating in St. Helena

BLACKBERRY OR OTHER
FRUIT COBBLER
ANNE CUTTING AND SUE CROSS

This easy to make treat is great any time of year with fresh fruit or frozen berries. One can make it putting cobbler mixture on top of fruit or fruit on top of mixture. Try it with peaches, nectarines, plums or apricots.

2/3 cube butter
1 cup sugar
1 cup flour
2 teaspoons baking powder
3/4 cup milk
3 cups blackberries

Melt butter in an 8" square glass baking dish. Mix sugar, flour, baking powder and milk. Mush fruit in melted butter and cover with above mixture. Bake 350° 35 minutss.

TIN ROOF SUNDAE SAUCE
VALERIE PRESTEN

Originally from 1982 Private Stock Cookbook published by the United Airlines Friendship Guild for the Children's Orthopedic Hospital and Medical Center, Seattle WA. The recipe is called Fudge Nut Sauce, but I call it Tin Roof Sundae Sauce.

1 cup butter or margarine
2 cups semi-sweet chocolate chips
1 cup chopped Spanish peanuts
(to make Tin Roof Sundae)
1 teaspoon vanilla

In a double boiler over hot water, melt butter or margarine and chocolate chips, stirring until smooth. Stir in the nuts and vanilla. Serve hot over ice cream, top with a sprinkling of Spanish peanuts. You can substitute other nuts – walnuts, pecans, whatever you like. The sauce hardens on ice cream – just like outside of an ice cream bar or dipped cone. Makes 2 cups sauce.

CHOCOLATE SHEET CAKE
SALLY TANTAU, BETTY BECKSTOFFER, ALICE JONES, SYLVIA PESTONI, SARAH SIMPSON

As you see this was a popular cake in its day – everyone asked for the recipe. A life saver. Looks like brownies, but has consistency of sour cream cake.

2 cups sugar
2 cups flour
5 tablespoons cocoa
1 teaspoon baking soda
1 teaspoon cinnamon (optional)
1 cup water
2 cubes butter
1/2 cup solid shortening
2 eggs
1/2 cup buttermilk
1 teaspoon vanilla
1 tablespoon rum (optional)

Preheat oven to 400°. Mix together sugar, flour, cocoa, cinnamon and baking soda. Add eggs, buttermilk, vanilla and rum to flour mixture. Bring water, butter and shortening to a rapid boil. Pour hot liquid into batter. Mix and pour into a greased and floured sheet cake pan 12" x 17". Bake 15 to 20 minutes.

ICING
1 pound powdered sugar, sifted
4 tablespoons cocoa
1 teaspoon vanilla
1 cube butter, melted
5 tablespoons milk or buttermilk

Mix together icing ingredients and spread on cake as soon as it comes from oven. This will create a glaze.

CHOCOLATE CAKE
CAROLYN PRIDE

Everyone's request for birthday cake and the 9" x 12" version always requested at pot lucks, etc. It was Sally's Chocolate Cake and Carolyn's Chocolate Frosting. I didn't like the frosting that came with the cake recipe. Nuts, sprinkled on top of frosting are optional.

2¼ cups flour
1/2 teaspoon salt
1 cube butter
1 pound brown sugar
2 eggs
2 squares chocolate, melted (2 ounces)
1/2 cup buttermilk
2 teaspoons vanilla
2 teaspoons baking soda
1 cup water, boiling

Preheat oven to 350°. Sift flour and salt and set aside. Cream butter and brown sugar together then add 2 eggs. Stir in melted chocolate, buttermilk and vanilla. Add dry ingredients. Add baking soda, which has been dissolved in boiling water. Batter will be thin. Grease and flour two 9" cake pans and bake 350° 30 minutes **OR** grease and flour a 9" x 12" x 2" pan and bake 375° 25 to 30 minutes.

CHOCOLATE BUTTER CREAM FROSTING
2 cups powdered sugar
1/4 cup butter
1 tablespoon milk
1 egg
1 teaspoon vanilla
1/8 teaspoon salt
2 squares melted chocolate

Eating in St. Helena

9½ MINUTE CAN'T FAIL HOLIDAY FRUITCAKE
SYD MENSCH

2½ cups sifted flour
1 teaspoon baking soda
2 eggs, lightly beaten
1 28-ounce jar mince meat
1 can sweetened condensed milk
1 cup coarsely chopped walnuts
2 cups mixed candied fruit

Butter 9" tube pan or spring form, line with waxed paper and butter again. Sift flour and baking soda. Combine eggs, mince meat, sweetened condensed milk, walnuts and fruits. Fold in dry ingredients then pour into pan. Bake 300° 2 hours until center springs back and top is golden. Cool. Turn out; remove paper. Decorate with walnuts and cherries.

BOB CRATCHIT'S CAKE
SYD MENSCH

1 cup brown sugar
1/2 cup butter, melted
1 cup mincemeat (ready to use)
1/2 cup raisins, more if you like
1/2 cup dates
2 eggs
1/2 cup chopped walnuts
1/2 cup applesauce
2 cups all purpose flour
1 tablespoon baking powder
1/2 teaspoon salt

Preheat oven to 350°. Mix together mincemeat, raisins, dates, nuts and applesauce. Add eggs, brown sugar and butter. Add combined flour, baking powder and salt. Mix thoroughly and pour into mold or loaf pan. Bake 350° 45 minutes or 325° 60 minutes. Cool and remove from pan while warm.

HARD SAUCE
1/2 cup butter, melted
1/2 cup powdered sugar
1/4 teaspoon lemon juice
1/4 teaspoon vanilla
Mix hard sauce ingredients and pour over warm cake.

BEST OLD FRUIT CAKE
SHIRLEY SPARKS

This recipe yields 17 pounds of fruitcake. Use many small gift size pans or several large size loaf pans. You can substitute 4 pounds of prepared candied fruit for the citron, peels and candied pineapple.

1 pound blanched almonds (3 cups)
1/2 pound pecans (2 cups)
1 pound walnuts (3 cups)
1 pound citron, cut into strips
1/2 pound lemon peel
1/2 pound orange peel
1 cup candied pineapple
1 pound candied cherries
2 pounds seeded raisins
1 pound dry figs (2 cups)
1 pound pitted dates (2 cups)
1 glass brandy
1 cup blackberry jam
4 teaspoons cinnamon
1/2 teaspoon allspice
2 teaspoon nutmeg
1/2 teaspoon cloves
1 pound butter
1 pound brown sugar
1 cup molasses
1 dozen eggs, beaten until foamy
1 pound flour (3½-4 cups)
2 teaspoons salt
whole candied cherries
whole blanched almonds for decoration

Chop nuts and fruits; this may be done in food processor, as it's very sticky. Combine and add brandy, jam and spices; mix well. Cream butter, add sugar, molasses and beaten eggs, mix thoroughly; add flour and salt; mix well. Pour over fruit mixture. Dough should be fairly stiff. If too stiff add more brandy. Grease pans well and line with heavy waxed or parchment paper. Grease again. Fill pans 3/4 full. Put pan of water in oven for moisture. Bake 300° 2-3 hours depending on size until tester comes out clean. Decorate tops before baking. When done, turn cakes on racks to cool. Pour a little brandy slowly over each cake. Wrap each cake in Saran-wrap and store for several weeks until Christmas. Spray on more brandy as needed during the holiday season.

MAMA FRANK'S ICE BOX CAKE
HEIDI VIERA

In going through my mother's recipes I came across this "archive" recipe of my great grandmother's, Mrs. John A Wheeler (1918-1948.) She lived in the large stone house on the southwest corner of West Zinfandel Lane. This "ice box" cake was served at all the ladies luncheons and to family on special occassions. Can you imagine eating this rich dessert on top of a big family dinner. Oh my gosh, poetry would not even begin to describe me if I did. My mother's comment added to recipe, "Not on any diet I know."

1 cup butter
2 cups sugar
3 whole eggs
1/2 pound almonds, blanched and coarsly ground
3 eggs, separated
2 cups heavy cream, slightly whipped
20 lady fingers
20 almond macaroons

Cream butter and sugar well. Add whole eggs, beating well, beat in 3 extra egg yokes. Fold in almonds, cream and stiffly beaten egg whites. Line a long loaf pan with lady fingers and macaroons. Pour in mixture. Chill 24 hours. Serve with whipped cream and candied cherries. Freezes well. Serves 16.

APPLE CAKE
LINDA BERTOLI AND SARAH SIMPSON

Another wonderful recipe that has been passed around town – no one seems to know the source. Sarah's recipe is almost the same except she used shortening and 1 cup of nuts.

2 cups sugar
2 eggs
1/2 cup oil
2 teaspoons vanilla
2 cups flour
1 teaspoon salt
2 teaspoons cinnamon
2 teaspoons baking soda
1/2 cup chopped nuts
4 cups unpeeled and cut up apples
1/4 cup brandy or dark rum

Preheat oven to 350°. Beat eggs, sugar, brandy or rum, oil and vanilla. Sift flour with cinnamon and baking soda. Add to eggs and sugar. Mix well. Add apples and nuts. Bake in **metal** pan 45 minutes.

PUMPKIN CAKE
SHARON AND GEORGE STEINAUER

Bob's mother baked this cake during the Thanksgiving and Christmas holidays.

1 3/4 cups flour
1 tablespoon baking powder
3/4 teaspoon salt
2 teaspoons cinnamon
1/4 teaspoon cloves
3 tablespoons butter
1/3 cup shortening
1 2/3 cups sugar
2 eggs
3/4 cup cooked pumpkin
3/4 cup milk

Preheat oven to 350°. Sift flour, baking powder, salt and spices. Cream butter and shortening together. Add sugar gradually, creaming until light and fluffy. As eggs, one at a time, beating will after each. Add pumpkin and mix well. Add flour and milk alternately beating until smooth. Bake 1 hour or until done. Frost with cinnamon flavored butter cream. Serves 12.

PUMPKIN NUT BREAD
SYLVIA PESTONI

1 1/3 cups sugar
1 cup pumpkin puree
1/2 cup milk
2 eggs
1 2/3 cups all-purpose flour
1 teaspoon baking soda
2 teaspoons pumpkin pie spice
1/2 teaspoon salt
1/2 cup chopped nuts

Preheat oven to 350°. Blend first five ingredients in mixing bowl. Add remaining ingredients, beat at medium speed 1 minute. Turn into greased 5" x 9" loaf pan. Bake 60-65 minutes. Cool before slicing.

ZUCCHINI CAKE
PHOEBE ELLSWORTH

We all have too much zucchini mid summer and what's better than using it for a wonderful moist cake. This recipe came to me from neighbor Chrissy Young.

4 eggs
1½ cups oil
3 cups brown sugar
3 cups grated zucchini
2 teaspoons vanilla
3 cups flour
1½ teaspoons baking powder
1 teaspoon baking soda
1½ teaspoons cinnamon
1 teaspoon salt
1 cup chopped nuts

Preheat oven to 350°. Beat eggs until light yellow. Continue beating and add oil, vanilla, sugar and zucchini. Sift dry ingredients. Add to first mix and blend well. Add 1 cup chopped nuts. Bake in well greased bundt pan 90 minutes
NOTE For chocolate zucchini cake add 2 squares melted unsweetened chocolate.

PINEAPPLE NUT BREAD
SYD MENSCH

Moist and fruity….. Perfect with coffee or fruit salad

1¾ cups sifted all-purpose flour
2 teaspoons baking powder
1/2 teaspoon salt
1/4 teaspoon soda
1/2 cup raisins
3/4 cup chopped walnuts
3/4 cup sugar
3 tablespoons soft butter
2 eggs, unbeaten
1 8½-ounce can crushed pineapple, not drained

Preheat oven to 350°. Measure first four ingredients into sifter; set aside. Rinse raisins with boiling water to plump them; drain well; set aside with walnuts. Gradually beat sugar into butter. Beat in eggs, one at a time. Add raisins and nuts. Sift in about half the flour mixture; stir (don't beat) just until moistened and fairly smooth. Add pineapple with its syrup, then stir in rest of flour mixture. Quickly but gently spoon the heavy batter into greased 5" x 9" x 3" loaf pan. Sprinkle with a topping mixture of 2 tablespoons granulated sugar and 1/2 teaspoon cinnamon. Bake 350° 60 to 70 minutes or until done when tested. Turn out onto a rack.

PERSIMMON BREAD
LISSA MILLER

2 cups sugar
2 tablespoons butter
2 eggs
1 cup milk
2 cups persimmon pulp
2 teaspoons vanilla
2½ cups plus 1 tablespoon flour
1 teaspoon salt
2 teaspoons baking soda
2 teaspoons baking powder
1 cup raisins
1 cup chopped nuts, optional

Preheat oven to 350°. Cream sugar and butter together. Add eggs and milk. Add persimmon pulp and vanilla. Sift flour, salt, baking powder, and baking soda. Add to persimmon mixture. Blend well with mixer. Fold in raisins and nuts if used. Grease and line 2 regular sized loaf pans with wax or parchment paper and fill with mixture. Bake 90 minutes or until done. Check for doneness – this bread sometimes takes 2 hours. Remove from oven. Cool thoroughly on racks upside down. Remove paper. Wrap in foil. Refrigerate to keep fresh more than four days. This bread is very moist.

LEMON BREAD
CAROLYN PRIDE

From Colorado Cache, Junior League of Denver, 1998. This book has been one of my mainstays. This is fabulous. Best is that you have to make it at least a day ahead.

6 tablespoons butter
3/4 cup sugar
2 eggs
3 tablespoons lemon juice
2 teaspoons lemon peel, freshly grated
1½ cups flour, sifted
1 teaspoon salt
1/2 cup milk
1/2 cup chopped walnuts
GLAZE
3 tablespoons lemon juice
1/2 cup sugar

Preheat oven to 350°. Cream butter and 3/4 cup sugar until fluffy. Beat in eggs one at a time. Beat in 3 tablespoons lemon juice and lemon peel. Add flour that has been sifted with baking powder and salt alternately with milk, beating just enough to blend. Fold in walnuts. Line bottom of a greased 8" x 4" loaf pan with wax paper. Butter waxed paper and turn batter into pan. Bang pan down hard on work surface to settle dough. Bake at 350° 60 minutes or until toothpick comes out clean. Blend 3 tablespoons lemon juice and 1/2 cup sugar. Pour mixture slowly over hot bread. Let bread remain in pan until glaze is absorbed, at least 15 minutes.

IMPORTANT NOTE
Remove bread from pan, leaving on waxed paper. Let stand on rack until completely cooled. Remove wax paper, wrap bread in foil and let sit 24 hours before serving.

Eating in St. Helena

Favorite Cookbooks and Food Magazines

LEONA AVES

For years and years my favorite food magazine was *Bon Appetite*. Then I switched to *Cooks' Illustrated,* now I don't subscribe to any magazines. I do watch the cooking shows on TV and *Paula Deen* is one of my favorites.

KATHY AND MIKE CHELINI

Our coffee table is always covered with food and wine magazines from *Saveur*, *Gourmet*, and *Food and Wine*, but we cook to our own taste and family traditions. We love our cookbooks, but lately we have referred to *Cooks' Illustrated* and have learned a few tricks from Mario Batali and Judy Rogus at Zuni Café.

SUE CROSS

Make it Now, Bake it Later
James Beard's cookbooks (all)
Fanny Farmer's Bible
Elena's Fiesta Recipes
Maggie Gin, Regional *Cooking of China*
Winemakers' Recipes – spiral bound

We loved

Aunt Jemima's Coffee Cake Mix
Aunt Jemima's Corn Bread Mix
 (My grandchildren still like these)
Lawry's Spaghetti Sauce Mix
 *(Scary, when we made real spaghetti
  sauce it tasted weird.)*
Lawry's Taco Mix
All MSG – good!
Toll House Cookies
 *(We ate most of the batter before we
  baked the cookies!)*
When one peach tree was a perfect ripeness, we made hand-cranked peach ice cream with cream – of course it was perfect.

HELEN WALKA DAKE

I used *Joy of Cooking*, the *Sunset* paperback books, *Silver Palate*, with an occasional foray into *Julia Child* (but not for family cooking). One my most well-worn books is Mirelle Johnson's *Cuisine of the Sun*, especially for main dish omelets. One of my recipes comes from Francine Allen's, *Eating Well in a Busy World*, another favorite cookbook.

MARYBETH EGNER

Joy of Cooking, *Better Homes and Gardens New Cookbook*, *Betty Crocker*, Emily Chase's,*The Pleasures of Cooking with Wine and Sunset Magazine.*

PHOEBE ELLSWORTH

Joy of Cooking, *San Francisco Junior League Cookbook*, *Sunset Magazine*, *San Francisco Chronicle and Napa Register* food sections, Peg Bracken's, *I Hate to Cook Book*, Wine Institute's, *Favorite Recipes of California Winemakers,* Angelo Pelegrini's, *UnPrejudiced Palate and Americans by Choice*, and M.F.K. Fisher's books

VERA HAMPTON

I used *Sunset* and the *San Francisco Junior League Cookbook.* Mostly I used recipes I had collected from one source or another - newspapers, magazines etc. I can hardly read the recipe cards, they are so old. And now you can access *Epicurus*

SANDY HERRICK

As far as what my kids liked and didn't like mayo was poison in their minds, and still is!! One year when they were 6 and 9, I was so sick of whining about what we were having for dinner each night I informed them that they each had to cook one night each week. The night was assigned. They each had to tell me the night before what we were going to have and I would teach them to cook whatever it was they came up with. Nothing was off limits and basic food groups had to be included in some fashion. We had some pretty wild meals, especially from Heather, but we had so much fun and no more whining!!! They both enjoy cooking now, so I guess it was a good idea.

BETSY HOLZHAUER

In the winter I use *Soups for all Seasons*. I also like Marian Morash's, *The Victory Garden Cookbook*. *Sunset* is the only magazine I've ever saved and used recipes.

DIANE LIVINGSTON

Mildred Knopf's, *Cook My Darling Daughter*
Houston Junior League Cookbook – given to me by Lucy Shaw
Pasadena Prefers- recommended by Lucy Shaw

SYLVIA PESTONI

Joy of Cooking, *Betty Crocker* (yes Betty Crocker), any book by *Alice Waters*, *Silver Palete*, *San Francisco Junior League A La Carte*, *Gourmet*, *Bon Appetite*, *Cooks, and Cuisine*

VALERIE PRESTEN

As for cookbooks/magazines I've used most over the years – that's a bit difficult because I use so many. In fact, someone once told me, "Valerie, the only thing wrong with your cooking is that you rarely make the same dish twice." I'm lucky to be married to an adventuresome eater (helps since his mother (God rest her soul) was a terrible cook.) I have wonderful cooks in my family. My mother was a great cook, and we all like to eat! However, if you pinned me down, there are some cookbooks I can always count on: *Cotton Country Collection*, Judith Ets-Hokin's, *San Francisco Dinner Party Cookbook*, *Betty Crocker*, *Silver Palate*, *The Best of Regional Thai Cuisine*, *Cook Malaysia*, and *By Request*.

CAROLYN PRIDE

First of all, every bride in the 1950"s received a *Joy of Cooking*, sometimes multiple copies. It was our Bible. Thinking back I remember doing a lot with Campbell's Cream of Tomato soup or Mushroom or Celery, etc. It seemed that at least once a month a new recipe, usually for a casserole was circulating, and we tried them all. I think my favorite all-time fail-safe cookbook is *Denver Junior League's, Creme de Colorado*, 1st Edition 1987, To this day I reach for it when company is coming.

JUDIE ROGERS

Married in 1955 my first cookbook was Betty Crocker's, *Good and Easy Cookbook*, newly published in 1954. It was divided into four sections -Breakfast, Lunch, Dinner , and the Fourth Meal (Coffee Get-Togethers, Afternoon Teas, Dessert Parites and so on.) No longer used, it still has a special place on my cookbook shelf with longtime favorites, the *Joy of Cooking* and the *Art of Eating*.

BARBARA SHURTZ

I love to read recipes and clip them out from newspapers. You can't clip the same way from the computer. I have saved recipes from *San Jose Mercury*, *San Francisco Chronicle* and *Napa Register*. Also, favorites came from *Sunset* magazines and cookbooks, as well as *Better Homes and Gardens*. Later, came *Gourmet*, *Bon Appetit*, *Joy of Cooking* and many other cookbooks.

DIANA STOCKTON

James, Beard, *The James Beard Cookbook*
    Basically, stick an onion with several
    cloves and get on with whatever it is.
Alice May Brock, *Alice's Restaurant Cookbook*
    Never not cook something because you
    don't have the right pan. Don't worry
    about measuring spoons and cups.
Craig Claiborne, *New York Times Cookbook*
    Especially for soups.
Adelle Davis, *Let's Eat Right to Keep Fit*
    Use whole grains, stone ground flours:
    make your own baby food. Avoid
    anything instant or quick.
Margaret B.Lettvin, *Maggie's Back Book*
    Reaching for cans and cast iron skillets
    keeps one in shape. Store some
    on shoulder high shelves.
Irma S. Rombauer, *Joy of Cooking*
    What is, what to do with it.

LOIS SWANSON

Besides the tried and true books of *Betty Crocker*, and *Joy of Cooking*, I like *The Best Recipe Book*, and the quarterly magazine called *Eating Well* (eatingwell.com).

PAULA YOUNG

I did use and still do use many of *Sunset's* recipes. Two other favorite sources were recipes from *Allied Arts* in Menlo Park and any *Junior League* cookbook, but I do have definite favorites. Regarding Allied Arts, my friends and I would go there for special occasions. One could purchase the recipes that were served that day on blue index cards. The recipes were delicious and simple. Both my daughters and I love regional cooking and tend towards comfort food so we do love certain *Junior League* cookbooks a great deal. Of course, *Seattle's Simply Classic* and Hawaii's, *A Taste of Aloha* and *Another Taste of Aloha* are REAL favorites, maybe because we love fish so much.

INDEX

Eating in St. Helena

Sauces and Condiments

CONTRIBUTORS

LEONA AVES
BETTY BECKSTOFFER
LYNETTE BENSEN
LINDA BERTOLI
KATA BROWNELL
ANN CARPY
KATHY CARRICK
SYLVIA CENDJAS
KATHY AND MIKE CHELINI
KATHY COLLINS
SUE CROSS
ANNE CUTTING
KAREN DAHL
HELEN DAKE
JAMIE DAVIES
MARIE DEL BONDIO
MARJ DIXON
MISSY DORAN
SUSAN EDELEN
MARYBETH EGNER
PHOEBE ELLSWORTH
SUE FOGARTY
DIANNE FRASER
THERESE FREY
SARAH GALBRAITH
NANCY GARDEN
HELEN GHIRINGHELLI NELSON
LADDIE HALL
VERA HAMPTON
INGE HEINEMANN
SANDY HERRICK
BETSY HOLZHAUER
TONI NICHELINI IRWIN
ALICE JONES
CONNIE KAY
DIANE LIVINGSTON
MARCIA MAHER'S FAMILY
ANTONIO MANZO FAMILY
MARY ANN MCCOMBER
WILLINDA MCCREA
SEANA MCGOWAN
SYD MENSCH
LISSA MILLER

JANICE MONDAVI
DONNA MORGAN
NANCY MORRELL
MARY NOVAK
JOHN NYQUIST
SIENA O'CONNELL
MARIE OLIVER
CAROLE PARR
TERESE PARRIOTT
BECKY PARRIOTT
KATHLEEN PATTERSON
SYLVIA PESTONI
MARIANNE PETERSEN
SANDRA PICKETT
BEV POPKO
RICK POPKO
VALERIE PRESTEN
CAROLYN PRIDE
ANN PUTNAM
GERI RAYMOND
VIRGINIA RAYMOND
JUDIE ROGERS
BARBARA RYAN
RUTHIE RYDMAN
BARBARA SHAFER
LUCY SHAW
BARBARA SHURTZ
SARAH SIMPSON
SUSAN SMITH
SHIRLEY SPARKS
BARBARA STANTON
SHARON AND GEORGE STEINAUER
DIANA STOCKTON
LORAINE STUART
LOIS SWANSON
SALLY TANTAU
HAROLYN THOMPSON
EVALYN TRINCHERO
PATTY VASCONI
HEIDI VIERA
JOAN WESTGATE
BILL YOUNG
PAULA YOUNG
SHERLYN ZUMWALT

NAPA VALLEY COOKBOOKS FROM THE PAST

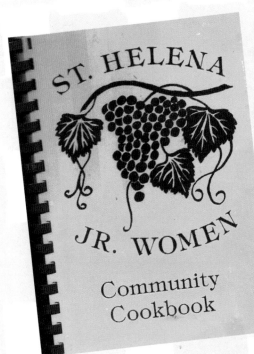

ST. HELENA JR. WOMEN Community Cookbook

The Very Finest Fresh Tomato Sauce In the Entire History of Mankind

by
George Stratton

A BOOK OF FAVORITE Recipes

Compiled by
FEDERATED WOMEN'S IMPROVEMENT CLUB
of
ST. HELENA
1978

"The Best in Cooking" in ST. HELENA

ST. HELENA BAND BOOSTERS CLUB
St. Helena, California

Vintage Cook with Emb...

Harvest Sip & Sample St. Helena

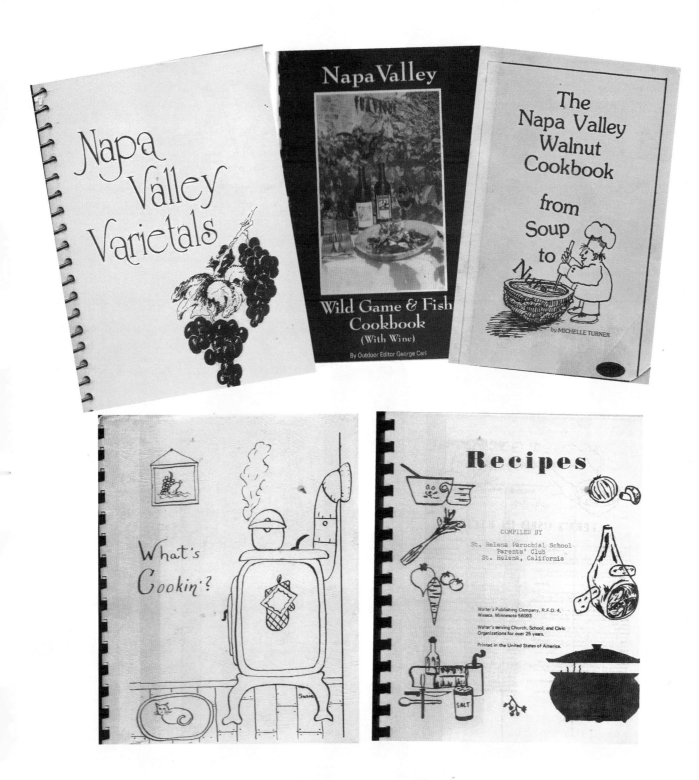

Cookbooks unearthed by
Marilyn Coy, Helen Dake, Helen Ghiringhelli Nelson, Toni Nichelini Irwin,
Sandra Pickett, Barbara Shurtz and Diana Stockton

Made in the USA
Charleston, SC
06 January 2011